Bartending doesn't *have* to be a mystery!

With THE CONCISE BAR GUIDE by your side, you can master the skills of a professional bartender at your own home bar.

Learn the secrets of a successful party; how to stock your bar; guidelines for choosing wines; tips for hosting large and small gatherings; recipes for hundreds of drinks—from traditional to trendy; selecting barware and appropriate glassware; serving nonalcoholic drinks; tips on preparing snacks and hors d'oeuvres; and much more!

Also From The Berkley Publishing Group

BAR TRICKS
THE COMPLETE BARTENDER

THE CONCISE BAR GUIDE

E. Edward Williams

BERKLEY BOOKS, NEW YORK

THE CONCISE BAR GUIDE

A Berkley Book/published by arrangement with
Boldface Publishing, Inc.

PRINTING HISTORY
Berkley edition/November 1990

ISBN: 0-425-12794-X

Contents

1. Introduction 1
2. Basic Bar Equipment 2
3. Stocking Your Bar 4
4. Mixed Drinks 7
5. Unmixed Drinks 8
6. Food with Drinks 12
7. Drink Recipes 15
8. Cautionary Wisdom 98
9. Alcohol-Free Drinks 101
   Glossary 106
   Measurement Conversions 109
   Index of Drinks by Ingredient 111
   Topic Index 119

THE CONCISE BAR GUIDE

1. Introduction

Whether you're mixing a single after-dinner drink for your own enjoyment or you've been elected bartender for the next family reunion, you should have a simple, easy-to-use guide for mixing drinks.

Recipes for all the classic and most of the currently popular cocktails are listed alphabetically in Chapter 7 and are cross-referenced by type of liquor in the index. Also included are some suggestions and recipes for snacks to accompany your drinks.

But before you jump into the recipes and start making drinks, it would be worth your while to read the chapters on stocking your bar, basic equipment and techniques, and the selection of glassware. A little knowledge about the finer points of bartending will increase your confidence as a bartender and enhance your guests' enjoyment of your hospitality.

Today, as we learn more about alcohol use and abuse, it is important to give some thought to your social responsibilities as a host. This topic is covered in Chapter 8.

So sit back, page through this book, think about having a few friends over, and enjoy!

2. Basic Bar Equipment

A well-equipped kitchen will already have most of the tools required for the well-equipped bar. You may want to purchase other items listed below if you are a first-time bartender or if you plan to entertain regularly:

- Cocktail shaker
- Blender
- Bar spoon and measuring spoons
- Measuring cups
- Swizzle sticks
- Shot glasses
- Strainer
- Cutting board
- Knife
- Water pitcher
- Toothpicks
- Napkins
- Straws
- Coasters
- Corkscrew
- Can and bottle openers
- Bar towels

- Tray
- Ice bucket and tongs

Glassware

Using the correct glass—and needless to say, using glass rather than plastic—adds greatly to the appeal of any drink. Perfectly adequate glassware is available at any discount store; it is not necessary to buy dozens of specialty glasses in different sizes and shapes. You can get by with four basic types of glass for all but the most formal events: cocktail glasses, old fashioned glasses, wineglasses, and collins glasses.

Cocktail and old fashioned glasses are used most often for mixed drinks. The cocktail glass is the classic stemmed glass holding about four ounces; the old fashioned glass is a short glass holding about eight ounces.

As for wineglasses, traditionalists will use a smaller glass for white wine and a larger bowl-shaped glass for red wine, but if you split the difference and get a moderate-size (10 oz.) glass you can get by with one size.

The other popular and versatile glass is the collins glass, a tall glass holding 10 to 14 ounces. It might be considered an all-purpose glass, since it is well suited to soft drinks, juices, and other beverages served over ice.

If you or your guests enjoy beer, you may want one or more sets of specialty beer glasses: mugs, schooners, or footed pilsner glasses.

You also might want to own brandy snifters, liqueur glasses, or champagne glasses (saucers or flutes). Small snifters are good to have if you're just beginning a bar, because they can also be used for cordials and liqueurs.

Here again, consider the type of entertaining you do and the kind of drinks you prefer. If you serve a lot of cordials, you may want to invest in cordial glasses. If you drink mainly wine, you may want several styles of wineglasses.

Party glasses should sparkle. If you wash your glasses in a dishwasher, make sure they are free of water spots. Rinse the glasses and dry them with a clean, lint-free towel.

Beer glasses should be given special attention: any soap residue will make the beer go flat. To avoid this, rinse the beer glasses in salt water after washing.

3

3. Stocking Your Bar

How you stock your bar will depend to a great extent on your life-style. If you will be entertaining close friends, you probably have a good idea which drinks they regularly enjoy, and you can stock your bar accordingly.

If you are planning to throw a large party or a special event, such as an anniversary reception or a retirement party, you should stock enough different ingredients to allow you to please a wide range of tastes. Some thought and a few inquiries may give you some idea of what types of drinks your guests favor.

In deciding what kind of liquor to buy, you might find it helpful to know that the ten most-often-ordered drinks are:

1. Vodka and tonic
2. Gin and tonic
3. Rum and Coke
4. Bloody Mary
5. Beer
6. White wine
7. Margarita
8. Martini
9. Manhattan
10. Long Island Iced Tea

To be safe, stock your bar with all the major liquors, a few well-chosen liqueurs, beer, wine, and a variety of mixers.

Basic Stock

Liquors: Vodka, gin, rum, brandy, tequila, scotch, and bourbon or a blended whiskey.

Liqueurs: Baileys Original Irish Cream, Kahlúa, triple sec, Galliano, amaretto, crème de cacao, crème de menthe, Drambuie, Sambuca.

Beer: A popular brand, a light beer, and possibly an import and a nonalcoholic beer.

Wine: You will certainly want to have white wine on hand, and perhaps some red. Many people choose to drink wine or a wine spritzer rather than hard liquor.

Alcoholic mixers: Sweet and dry vermouth.

Nonalcoholic mixers: Club soda, mineral water, tonic, cola, sour mix, juices (orange, tomato, cranberry, grapefruit), Rose's lime juice, bitters. Get plenty of these mixers, along with some diet soda.

Other ingredients: Heavy cream, fresh lemons and limes, grenadine syrup, sugar, Tabasco and Worcestershire sauce, olives, cocktail onions, and cherries. Many recipes call for sugar syrup, which can be bought ready made, or prepared by boiling a pint of water with a pound of sugar until sugar is dissolved.

How Much to Buy

Determining how much liquor to buy for a party is one of the toughest things for a new host to do. Generally it becomes easier with experience. To get a rough idea of what to buy, you need to do some guessing. First, make a guess at what most people will be drinking (beer, wine, mixed drinks). Then estimate how much they will be drinking—for example, less at a formal gathering, more at a lively party. Finally, decide about how long your party will last.

If you figure ten people will be drinking wine for two hours and will have two drinks an hour, you need (10 × 2 × 2) 40 servings of wine. A serving of wine is four ounces, so you need 160 ounces, or a four-liter and a one-liter bottle. (See Measurement Conversions at the back of this book.) For mixed drinks, figuring 1½ ounces of liquor per drink, a 750-milliliter bottle will make about 16 drinks.

Don't plan on more than two or three drinks an hour for each person. More than that will guarantee a problem with inebriated guests (see Chapter 8).

Ice

Ice is the one item many novice hosts mishandle. The most common mistake is not having enough ice; the second mistake is not having high-quality ice.

For anything more than the smallest party, you will need five or ten pounds of ice; that's one or two five-pound bags from the grocery or liquor store. If it's a summer or an outdoor party, you will need double or triple that amount.

If you are making your own ice, use bottled spring water so that your ice will be as clean and flavor-free as possible. Most commercial ice, especially the kind available in liquor stores, should serve you well.

Regular party-givers will want to buy an inexpensive ice chest, since even one bag of ice will fill up the average freezer compartment. The ice chest can double as a beer and wine cooler, since most people can't fit more than a couple of six-packs or bottles of wine into their refrigerator.

4. Mixed Drinks

Mixed drinks, as the name implies, contain two or more ingredients that must be mixed together. There are three basic ways to mix a drink: shaking, blending, and stirring.

Regardless of the method used to mix a drink, the ingredients are generally added in the same order: first the ice, then the liquor, and finally all other ingredients. Note that carbonated mixers such as soda or tonic are never shaken or blended, but are always stirred.

Shaking: Add ingredients to a cocktail shaker; shake with vigor for about 10 seconds; strain into a cocktail glass or into an old fashioned glass with fresh ice in it. Add garnish.

Blending: Blending is necessary when mixing solid or frozen ingredients such as chopped ice or ice cream to make a frozen drink. Most drinks which call for stirring can also be blended to make a frozen variety: blending a daiquiri with chopped ice makes a frozen daiquiri, and blending a Gold Cadillac with ice cream rather than cream makes a frozen Gold Cadillac, which is as much a dessert as an after-dinner drink.

To blend, add all ingredients to the blender container and blend for about a minute until drink reaches a smooth consistency.

Stirring: Pour all the ingredients, including carbonated mixers, into a glass and stir with a bar spoon or swizzle stick.

5. Unmixed Drinks

If guests ask for drinks "neat" or "straight," serve a shot of the requested liquor, with no ice or mixer, in an old fashioned glass. If a single liquor is requested "on the rocks" ("scotch on the rocks"), pour a shot over ice in an old fashioned glass. "With a splash of water (or soda)" means adding just enough mixer to take the bite off the first sip of liquor.

Beer and wine are also unmixed drinks. White wine should be served chilled, red wine at a cool room temperature. Many people like their beer served ice-cold, and this is no great loss with a light beer. Beers with a more complex flavor, such as imports, should be enjoyed much like wine: they should be served slightly chilled to allow enjoyment of the full flavor and bouquet of the beverage.

Since the appreciation of fine whiskeys, beers, and wines is becoming more widespread, some more detailed information on these drinks follows.

Whiskeys

While all whiskeys are made by the same method—taking a fermented brew, basically a beer, and distilling it—an almost infinite number of factors can change the flavor of the resulting liquor.

By tradition, and perhaps by an accident of geography, the

greatest variety of whiskeys, with the broadest range of flavors, is produced in Scotland. While the Scots and Canadians call their drink "whisky," in the United States and Ireland it's spelled "whiskey." Some excellent products are distilled in North America, notably bourbon, rye, Canadian whisky, and blended whiskey.

Single-malt scotch is made only from malted barley in a traditional, time-consuming, labor-intensive pot still.

Grain whiskey may be distilled from malted barley, but is more commonly made from corn and distilled in the faster, more automated continuous still.

Blended whiskeys are, as the name implies, a blend of single malt and grain whiskeys.

A blended scotch will contain at least two dozen different whiskeys, and the number could approach four dozen, including two or three different grain whiskeys. Premium blends will contain a greater percentage of the malt whiskeys, and these are the ingredients that give a blend most of its characteristic flavor.

Whiskeys draw their complex flavors from a number of variables: the water, the malt, and the still. Water from various sources can vary in hardness and flavor.

Bourbon must be distilled from 51 percent corn, but it also includes rye and barley malt. Blended whiskey can include other ingredients such as sherry or fruit juices. Canadian whisky is distilled primarily from rye and corn.

Any premium whiskey should be enjoyed as close to its natural state as possible: straight up or with just a splash of water. This is true of the good blends and imperative with the single malts. There's no point in buying premium whiskey for use in mixed drinks; get a cheaper blend for that.

Like wine or brandy, a good whiskey should be savored with all the senses. Enjoy the color, the aroma, the taste, and the aftertaste.

Beer

Beer making is an ancient endeavor that can be traced back to about 6000 B.C. Some historians go so far as to argue that man developed agricultural societies in order to cultivate the grain they needed to produce beer.

While early beers had the same base as today's brews—wheat, water, and yeast fermented to produce an alcoholic drink—the taste of the final drink was much different because of the flavoring agents used. These ancient beers were flavored with a variety of herbs and were sometimes sweetened with honey or fruits.

Beer as we know it developed sometime around the ninth century with the use of hops as the dominant flavoring agent. Hops give beer its slightly bitter taste and were used partly because they acted as a natural preservative, an important benefit in the centuries before pasteurization and refrigeration.

There are two major categories of beer, depending on the type of yeast used in the brewing process. "Bottom-fermentation" beers are made with a type of yeast that works at lower temperatures for a longer fermentation time. "Top-fermentation" beers use a variety of yeast that works more quickly at a higher temperature.

Some of the major types of beer are:

Ale. This top-fermented brew has a darker color than lager beer and often has more of the bitter taste of hops.

Bock Beer. This bottom-fermentation beer is dark in color with a strong, malty, somewhat sweet taste.

Creme Ale. A blend of ale and lager beer that is highly carbonated.

Dark Beer. The addition of roasted barley in early brewing stages gives dark beer its deep color and full, creamy taste; this is a bottom-fermentation beer.

Lager. Essentially the same as pilsner, a lighter bottom-fermented beer.

Malt Liquor. An American beer with a higher alcohol content (generally over 5 percent) and a malty taste.

Pilsner. Named after the Bohemian city of Pilsen, where this kind of beer was first brewed. A light golden bottom-fermented beer with a crisp, clean taste.

Porter. A very dark, bitter top-fermented beer.

Stout. A dark, creamy beer similar to porter; an example is Guinness.

Weisse Beer. A beer brewed with a percentage of wheat in addition to the barley.

A common mistake in serving beer is to serve it too cold. Like wine, beer releases more of its flavor and aroma at a cool but not ice-cold temperature. Most beers should be served at about 45 degrees.

Soap residue in a beer glass will kill the head, so before using a beer glass that has been washed with soap, rinse it with salt water.

Wine

Like beer, wine has an ancient history, dating back thousands of years to its roots in the Mediterranean area. Wine is made primarily from grapes, which are picked at their ripest in the fall and crushed and further pressed to remove all stems and skins, leaving only the juice. The juice is then allowed to ferment in vats under the influence of its own or supplemental yeasts. The resulting wine is then filtered and put into bottles, or into casks for aging and later bottling.

In broadest terms, you might say there are two kinds of wine: white and red. But beyond this simple division is an endless variety of wines, ranging from the blush wines, which are something of a combination of red and white wines, to far more subtle categories, such as grape varieties, growing regions, and vintages. And within all these classifications are further distinctions based on taste, aroma, and color. The subject of wines and their types is too broad and too complex to be addressed in detail in this book, but if you want to become more informed about fine wines and imported vintages, there are many good books available at your library or bookstore.

Some of the more familiar white wines are Chablis, chardonnay, Chenin Blanc, Fumé Blanc, and Riesling.

Red wines you may wish to become familiar with include burgundy, cabernet sauvignon, Chianti, Pinot Noir, and zinfandel.

For casual drinking most people today prefer a fairly dry white wine such as a chardonnay, Fumé Blanc, or white burgundy.

For drinking with meals, the rule of thumb has always been to drink white wines with lighter dishes such as seafood and poultry and red wines with heavier meats such as beef and pasta. Increasingly, however, even wine experts are beginning to drink what they enjoy most. If you want to drink a light red wine with your chicken, go ahead and enjoy it!

Wine can also be enjoyed with desserts, although it is wise to avoid overly sweet treats. A light white, such as a sauterne, would go well with light desserts. A somewhat stronger wine, perhaps a port, could be paired with a chocolate dessert.

Generally, as mentioned earlier, white wines should be served chilled, but red wines taste best at a cool room temperature.

6. Food with Drinks

Food served during a cocktail party should be as simple as possible. The less time you need to spend in the kitchen during your party, the more time you will have to enjoy the company of your guests.

Plan foods that can be made in advance and served without a great deal of effort. Good choices for simple parties are chips, nuts, raw vegetables, dips, spreads, cheese, crackers, and breads.

For more elaborate parties and cocktail buffets you might want to add cold sliced ham, roast beef, and turkey or cold cooked shrimp with cocktail sauce.

For a spur-of-the-moment or effortless party, you can buy prepared dips and spreads, but to save money and get better quality you will want to make your own.

Basic Dip and Spread

To make a basic dip for vegetables, chips, or crackers, start with a carton of sour cream. (For a lower fat and calorie substitute, put low-fat cottage cheese and a little lemon juice in a blender or food processor and mix until it's the consistency of sour cream—use 1 tbsp. lemon juice to every lb. of cottage cheese.) Then simply add your favorite ingredients to achieve a taste you like: chives, dill, dry onion soup mix, horseradish and bacon bits, chopped clams, or shrimp.

To make a cheese spread, soften some cream cheese and mix in finely chopped onion, green pepper, carrot, and herbs, or try your own variations.

Recipes

To get you started, here are some recipes for dips and spreads—some old favorites and some new. Enjoy!

Three Cheese Spread

8 oz. bleu cheese
8 oz. finely grated cheddar cheese
8 oz. cream cheese
3 tbsp. grated onion
1½ tsp. Worcestershire sauce

Soften and thoroughly combine cheeses. Add all other ingredients and mix until smooth. Chill before serving as a dip or spread with a variety of crackers.

Easy Shrimp Treat

8 oz. cream cheese
  Seafood cocktail sauce
1 small can cocktail shrimp, drained and rinsed

Spread softened cheese into a circle on a medium-size plate. Top with the cocktail sauce, then with the shrimp. Serve with crackers and breads.

Guacamole

2 ripe avocados
1 tbsp. lemon juice
1/2 tsp. chili powder
2–3 garlic cloves, crushed
1/2 tsp. salt

Pit, peel, and mash the avocados. Mix in all other ingredients.
For a creamier guacamole, stir in some mayonnaise or sour
cream. If you like chunky guacamole, add a diced tomato, a
chopped hard-boiled egg, and 1/2 cup chopped black olives.
Serve with tortilla chips.

Hummus

1 16 oz. can chick-peas (garbanzos)
1/2 cup tahini (sesame seed paste)
1/3 cup lemon juice
3 garlic cloves
Dash cayenne
Dash soy sauce

Purée chick-peas in blender or food processor. Add all other
ingredients and mix into a smooth paste. Serve with wedges of
pita bread or with raw vegetables. **Note:** You will find tahini in
the ethnic foods section of your supermarket or at a Middle
Eastern grocery or a health food store. Garlic lovers can add
more garlic.

7. Drink Recipes

Abbey Cocktail

1½ oz. gin
2 tbsp. orange juice
Dash orange bitters
Maraschino cherry

Shake liquids with ice and strain into a cocktail glass. Top with cherry.

Acapulco

1½ oz. rum
1½ oz. triple sec
1 tbsp. lime juice
1 tsp. sugar
1 tsp. egg white
Mint sprig

Shake first five ingredients with ice and strain into an old fashioned glass. Top with mint sprig.

A.J.

1½ oz. applejack
1 oz. grapefruit juice

Shake well with ice and strain into a cocktail glass.

Alaska

1½ oz. gin
¾ oz. yellow Chartreuse
2 dashes orange bitters

Stir well with ice and strain into a cocktail glass.

Alfonso Cocktail

Dash Angostura bitters
1 tsp. sugar
1 oz. Dubonnet
Champagne

Combine bitters and sugar; add Dubonnet. Stir with an ice cube and fill cocktail glass with chilled champagne.

Allies

1 oz. gin
1 oz. dry vermouth
½ tsp. kümmel

Stir well with ice and strain into a cocktail glass.

American Beauty

¾ oz. brandy
¾ oz. dry vermouth

1 oz. orange juice
1/2 oz. crème de menthe
    Dash grenadine
1 oz. port

Combine all ingredients except port and shake well with ice.
Strain into a cocktail glass and float port on top.

Americano

---

3 oz. sweet vermouth
1 1/2 oz. Campari
    Orange peel

Stir liquids well with ice and strain into a cocktail glass. Garnish
with orange peel.

Apple Brandy Cocktail

---

1 1/2 oz. apple brandy
    1 tsp. grenadine
    1 tsp. lemon juice

Shake well with ice and strain into a cocktail glass.

Applejack Punch

---

2 quarts applejack
4 oz. grenadine
1 pint orange juice
2 quarts ginger ale
    Orange and apple slices

Pour first three ingredients into a punch bowl over a large block
of ice. Pour in ginger ale. Add oranges and apples.

Apricot Lady

    rum
 ~~oz.~~ apricot brandy
 ½ tsp. triple sec
 1 tbsp. lime juice
 1 tsp. egg white
    Orange slice

Shake liquids well with ice and strain into an old fashioned glass.
Add several ice cubes and orange slice.

B&B

 ½ oz. Benedictine
 ½ oz. brandy

Pour the Benedictine into a cordial glass. Very slowly pour the
brandy on top of the Benedictine, maintaining separate layers.

Bacardi

 2 oz. Bacardi rum
 1 oz. gin
    Juice of one lime
 ½ tsp. sugar
    Dash grenadine

Shake well with ice and strain into a cocktail glass.

Baltimore Bracer

 1 oz. brandy
 1 oz. anisette
 1 egg white

Shake well with ice and strain into a cocktail glass.

Baltimore Eggnog

1 oz. brandy
1 oz. rum
1 beaten egg
1 tsp. powdered sugar
½ cup milk
¼ cup heavy cream

Shake well with ice and strain into a collins glass.

Banana Daiquiri

1½ oz. rum
½ oz. triple sec
1½ oz. lime juice
1 tsp. sugar
1 banana, peeled and cut into 1-inch chunks
1 cup crushed ice

Combine all ingredients in blender jar and blend at low speed until mixed. Blend at high speed to desired consistency. Pour into a champagne glass.

Banshee

¾ oz. crème de cacao
¾ oz. crème de banane
¾ oz. heavy cream

Shake well with ice and strain into a cocktail glass.

Barbary Coast

½ oz. gin
½ oz. rum
½ oz. scotch
½ oz. crème de cacao
½ oz. heavy cream

Shake well with ice and strain into a cocktail glass.

Barton Special

½ oz. applejack
¼ oz. whiskey
¼ oz. gin

Shake well with ice and strain into an old fashioned glass.

Beachcomber

Lime wedge
Sugar
1½ oz. rum
½ oz. triple sec
½ oz. lime juice
Maraschino cherry

Moisten rim of cocktail glass with lime wedge and dip rim in sugar. Shake liquid ingredients with ice and strain into glass. Top with cherry.

Beer Buster

1½ oz. vodka
Beer
Dash Tabasco sauce

Pour vodka into a highball glass and fill glass with beer. Add Tabasco sauce and stir.

Betsy Ross

1½ oz. brandy
1½ oz. port
½ oz. triple sec

Stir with ice and strain into a cocktail glass.

Between the Sheets

½ oz. brandy
½ oz. rum
½ oz. triple sec
2 tbsp. lemon juice

Shake well with ice and strain into a cocktail glass.

Black Hawk

1¼ oz. whiskey
1¼ oz. sloe gin
 Maraschino cherry

Stir liquids well with ice and strain into a cocktail glass. Top with cherry.

Black Russian

1½ oz. vodka
¾ oz. coffee-flavored liqueur

Pour over ice into an old fashioned glass.

Black Velvet

6 oz. ice-cold stout
6 oz. champagne

Slowly pour stout into a cold champagne glass. Carefully pour champagne on top of stout, taking care to keep the two liquids separate.

Blackjack

1 oz. coffee
1 oz. kirsch
1/2 oz. brandy

Shake well with ice and strain into an old fashioned glass. Add ice cubes.

Blanche

1 oz. anisette
1 oz. triple sec
1/2 oz. curaçao

Shake well with ice and strain into a cocktail glass.

Blood and Sand

1/2 oz. scotch
1/2 oz. cherry-flavored brandy
1/2 oz. sweet vermouth
1 tbsp. orange juice

Shake well with ice and strain into a cocktail glass.

Bloodhound

1 oz. gin
1/2 oz. dry vermouth
1/2 oz. sweet vermouth
Crushed strawberries

Shake liquids well with ice and strain into a cocktail glass. Put strawberries on top.

Bloody Mary

1½ oz. vodka
4 oz. tomato juice
½ tsp. Worcestershire sauce
½ tsp. lemon juice
Several drops Tabasco sauce
Salt and pepper
Celery stalk

Shake well over ice and strain into an old fashioned glass. Add several ice cubes and celery stalk.

Bobby Burns

1½ oz. scotch
1½ oz. sweet vermouth
1½ tsp. Benedictine
Lemon peel

Stir liquids well with ice and strain into a cocktail glass. Top with twist of lemon.

Boilermaker

1½ oz. blended whiskey
12 oz. beer

Drink the whiskey straight and then drink the beer. Some people prefer to add the whiskey to the beer and drink them together.

Bolero

1½ oz. rum
¾ oz. apple brandy
¼ tsp. sweet vermouth

Stir well with ice and strain into a cocktail glass.

Bombay

    1 oz. brandy
    ½ oz. sweet vermouth
    ½ oz. dry vermouth
    1–2 dashes curaçao
    1–2 dashes Pernod

Stir well with ice and strain into a cocktail glass.

Bombay Punch

    3 cups lemon juice
    1 cup powdered sugar, or to taste
    1 quart brandy
    1 quart dry sherry
    ½ cup triple sec
    ½ cup maraschino liqueur
    4 quarts champagne
    2 quarts club soda
      Orange slices (optional)

Dissolve sugar in lemon juice. Pour over a block of ice in a large punch bowl. Add all other ingredients, stir well. Add slices of seasonal fruit for color and taste.

Brandy Alexander

    ¾ oz. brandy
    ¾ oz. crème de cacao
    ¾ oz. heavy cream

Shake vigorously with ice. Strain into a cocktail glass.

Brandy Crusta

    ½ lemon
    1 tsp. sugar

2 oz. brandy
½ oz. triple sec
1 tsp. lemon juice
1 tsp. maraschino liqueur
Dash Angostura bitters
Orange slice
Maraschino cherry

Rub the edge of a cocktail glass with the lemon; then dip the rim into the sugar. Cut a spiral from the lemon rind and add it to the glass. Stir liquid ingredients well with ice. Strain into the glass and garnish with orange slice and cherry.

Brandy Daisy

2 oz. brandy
1 tsp. grenadine
½ tsp. powdered sugar
Juice of ½ lemon
Club soda (optional)
Orange slice

Shake first four ingredients with ice and strain into a large cocktail glass or goblet. Add chilled club soda if desired. Garnish with seasonal fruit.

Brandy Eggnog

2 oz. brandy
1 egg
1 tsp. powdered sugar
Milk
Nutmeg

Shake well with ice and strain into a collins glass. Fill the glass with milk and stir. Sprinkle with nutmeg.

Brandy Fix

1 tsp. powdered sugar
1 tsp. water
Juice of ½ lemon
2½ oz. brandy
Lemon slice

Dissolve sugar and water in a highball glass; add lemon juice and stir well. Add the brandy and lemon slice. Stir gently and serve with a straw.

Brandy Fizz

3 oz. brandy
Juice of ½ lemon
1 tbsp. powdered sugar
Juice of ¼ lime
Club soda

Shake first four ingredients well with ice and strain into a highball glass. Add ice cubes and fill glass with club soda.

Brandy Milk Punch

2 oz. brandy
1 tsp. powdered sugar
1 cup milk
Nutmeg

Shake first three ingredients well with ice and strain into a cocktail glass. Sprinkle with nutmeg.

Brandy Punch

Juice of 12 lemons
Juice of 4 oranges

½ cup superfine sugar
1 cup grenadine
1 quart club soda
2 quarts brandy
1 cup triple sec
1 pint cold tea

Add sugar to lemon and orange juice to sweeten to taste; then mix with the grenadine and club soda and pour over a large block of ice in a punch bowl; add remaining liquid ingredients, stir well, and garnish with seasonal fruits.

Brandy Sangaree

½ tsp. powdered sugar
1 tsp. water
2 oz. brandy
Club soda (optional)
Nutmeg

Dissolve powdered sugar in water and add brandy. Pour into a highball glass over ice. Fill glass with club soda if desired. Sprinkle with nutmeg.
Variation: Float three tablespoons port on top of the club soda before adding the nutmeg.

Brandy Sour

2 oz. brandy
Juice of ½ lemon
1 tsp. powdered sugar
Lemon or orange slice
Maraschino cherry

Shake first three ingredients well with ice and strain into a sour glass. Garnish with lemon or orange slice and maraschino cherry.

Brighton Punch

¾ oz. bourbon
¾ oz. brandy
¾ oz. Benedictine
2 tbsp. lemon juice
2 tbsp. orange juice
   Club soda
   Orange slices
   Lemon slices

Shake first five ingredients well with ice and strain into a collins glass filled with shaved ice. Fill glass with club soda and garnish with orange and lemon slices.

Broken Spur

2 oz. port
½ oz. gin
½ oz. sweet vermouth
½ tsp. triple sec

Shake well with ice and strain into a cocktail glass.

Bronx Cocktail

1½ oz. gin
½ oz. sweet vermouth
½ oz. dry vermouth
2 tbsp. orange juice
   Orange slice

Shake liquids well with ice and strain into a cocktail glass. Garnish with orange slice.

Bronx Silver

1 oz. gin
½ oz. dry vermouth

1 egg white
3 tbsp. orange juice

Shake well with ice and strain into a sour glass.

Buck's Fizz

1 cup fresh orange juice
1 bottle chilled champagne

Combine in a large pitcher and stir. Serve in tall glasses.

Bull's Milk

1½ oz. brandy
1 oz. light rum
1 tsp. powdered sugar
1 cup milk
Dash nutmeg
Dash cinnamon

Shake first four ingredients well with ice and strain into a collins glass. Sprinkle with nutmeg and cinnamon.

Cabaret Cocktail

1½ oz. gin
2 dashes bitters
½ tsp. dry vermouth
¼ tsp. Benedictine
Maraschino cherry

Stir liquids well with ice and strain into a cocktail glass. Top with cherry.

Cablegram

3 oz. rye
1 tsp. powdered sugar
Juice of ½ lemon
Club soda or ginger ale

Stir first three ingredients well with ice and strain into a highball glass. Fill glass with club soda or ginger ale.

Café de Paris

2 oz. gin
1 tsp. Pernod
1 tsp. heavy cream
1 egg white

Shake well with ice and strain into a cocktail glass.

Cape Codder

1½ oz. vodka
3 oz. cranberry juice
Lime slice

Stir liquids well with ice and strain into a highball glass. Add lime slice.

Capri

¾ oz. crème de cacao
¾ oz. crème de banane
¾ oz. light cream

Shake well over ice and strain into an old fashioned glass. Add fresh ice cubes.

Cara Sposa

1 oz. coffee-flavored brandy
1 oz. triple sec
½ oz. light cream

Shake well over ice and strain into a cocktail glass.

Cardinal Punch

3 cups lemon juice
½ cup powdered sugar
1 pint brandy
1 pint rum
1 bottle champagne, chilled
2 quarts red wine
1 quart carbonated water
1 cup sweet vermouth

Sweeten the lemon juice with powdered sugar. Pour into a punch bowl over a large block of ice. Add remaining ingredients. Stir well. Garnish with seasonal fruits.

Carrol

1½ oz. brandy
¾ oz. sweet vermouth
    Maraschino cherry

Stir well with ice and strain into a cocktail glass. Top with cherry.

Casablanca

2 oz. light rum
1½ tsp. triple sec
1½ tsp. lime juice
1½ tsp. maraschino liqueur

Shake well with ice and strain into a cocktail glass.

Champagne Cocktail

1 cube sugar
3 or 4 dashes Angostura bitters
    Champagne
    Lemon peel

Drop the sugar cube into a champagne glass and soak it with the bitters. Add cold champagne and stir gently. Garnish with a lemon peel.

Champagne Cup

1 bottle champagne, chilled
2 oz. brandy
2 oz. triple sec
4 tsp. powdered sugar
2 cups club soda
    Fruit
    Mint sprigs

Stir liquids well over ice in a large glass pitcher. Garnish with seasonal fruit; top with mint sprigs.

Champagne Punch

3 cups lemon juice
    Powdered sugar
1 pint brandy
1 cup triple sec
1 cup maraschino liqueur
2 bottles champagne, chilled
2 cups club soda

Sweeten lemon juice with powdered sugar; pour into a punch bowl over block of ice. Stir well; add remaining ingredients. Garnish with seasonal fruits.

Chapala

1½ oz. tequila
1 tbsp. lemon juice
1 tbsp. orange juice
½ tsp. triple sec
2 tsp. grenadine
Orange slice

Shake liquids well with ice and strain into an old fashioned glass.
Add ice cubes and orange slice.

Chapel Hill

2 oz. bourbon
¾ oz. triple sec
1 tbsp. lemon juice
Orange peel

Shake liquids well with ice and strain into a cocktail glass. Add
a twist of orange peel.

Cherry Blossom

1 oz. cherry-flavored brandy
Powdered sugar
1 oz. brandy
½ tsp. triple sec
½ tsp. grenadine
1 tsp. lemon juice
Maraschino cherry

Moisten the rim of a cocktail glass with some of the cherry-
flavored brandy and dip rim into powdered sugar. Shake liquid
ingredients well with ice and strain into the glass. Top with
cherry.

Chicago Fizz

1 oz. light rum
1 oz. port
3 tbsp. lemon juice
1 tsp. powdered sugar
1 egg white
Club soda

Shake first five ingredients well with ice and strain into a high-ball glass. Add ice cubes; fill glass with club soda. Stir well.

Chocolate Soldier

1½ oz. gin
¾ oz. Dubonnet
2 tbsp. lime juice

Shake well with ice and strain into a cocktail glass.

Claridge Cocktail

¾ oz. gin
¾ oz. dry vermouth
½ oz. apricot brandy
½ oz. triple sec

Stir well with ice and strain into a cocktail glass.

Classic Cocktail

1 lemon slice
1 tsp. powdered sugar
1 oz. brandy
½ oz. curaçao
½ oz. maraschino liqueur
1 tbsp. lemon juice

Moisten the rim of an old fashioned glass with the lemon slice and dip rim in the powdered sugar. Shake remaining ingredients well with ice and strain into the glass.

Clover Club Cocktail

1½ oz. gin
½ oz. grenadine
1 egg white
2 tbsp. lemon juice

Shake well with ice and strain into a cocktail glass.

Coffee Flip

1 oz. brandy
1 oz. port
1 tsp. powdered sugar
1 whole egg, thoroughly beaten
2 tsp. light cream
Nutmeg

Shake first five ingredients well with ice and strain into a cocktail glass. Sprinkle with nutmeg.

Cold Deck

1 oz. brandy
½ tsp. white crème de menthe
½ oz. sweet vermouth

Stir well with ice and strain into a cocktail glass.

Daiquiri

2 oz. light rum
1 tsp. powdered sugar
Juice of ½ lime

Shake well with ice and strain into a cocktail glass.

Damn-the-Weather Cocktail

1 oz. gin
1 tbsp. sweet vermouth
1 tbsp. orange juice
1 tsp. curaçao

Shake well with ice and strain into a cocktail glass.

Deauville Cocktail

½ oz. brandy
½ oz. applejack
½ oz. triple sec
1 tbsp. lemon juice

Shake well with ice and strain into a cocktail glass.

Dempsey Cocktail

1 oz. gin
1 oz. applejack
½ tsp. anisette
½ tsp. grenadine

Stir well with ice and strain into a cocktail glass.

Depth Bomb

1 oz. brandy
1 oz. apple brandy
Dash grenadine
Dash lemon juice

Shake with ice and strain into an old fashioned glass. Add ice.

Derby Daiquiri

1½ oz. light rum
1 oz. orange juice
1 tbsp. lime juice
1 tsp. sugar
½ cup crushed ice

Combine all ingredients in blender. Blend at low speed. Pour into a champagne flute.

Derby Fizz

2 oz. whiskey
1 tsp. triple sec
1 whole egg, thoroughly beaten
1 tsp. powdered sugar
Juice of ½ lemon
Club soda

Shake first five ingredients with ice and strain into a highball glass. Add ice cubes and fill glass with club soda. Stir.

Devil's Tail

2 oz. light rum
1 oz. vodka
1 tbsp. lime juice
1½ tsp. grenadine
1½ tsp. apricot brandy
½ cup crushed ice
Lime peel

Combine liquid ingredients in blender; blend at low speed and pour into a champagne flute. Add twist of lime.

Dinah Cocktail

1½ oz. whiskey
½ tsp. powdered sugar
1 tbsp. lemon juice
Mint sprig

Shake well with ice and strain into a cocktail glass. Top with mint sprig.

Dixie Cocktail

1 oz. gin
½ oz. dry vermouth
½ oz. Pernod
2 tbsp. orange juice

Shake well with ice and strain into a cocktail glass.

Dubonnet Cocktail

1½ oz. Dubonnet
1½ oz. gin
Dash orange bitters
Lemon peel

Stir liquids with ice and strain into a cocktail glass. Add twist of lemon.

Dubonnet Fizz

3 oz. Dubonnet
1 tsp. cherry-flavored brandy
2 tbsp. orange juice
1 tbsp. lemon juice
Club soda

Shake first four ingredients well with ice and strain into a highball glass. Add ice cubes and fill glass with club soda. Stir.

Duchess

1½ oz. Pernod
¾ oz. dry vermouth
¾ oz. sweet vermouth

Shake well with ice and strain into a cocktail glass.

Eggnog

2 oz. brandy
1 cup milk
1 egg
1 tsp. superfine sugar
2 or 3 dashes Angostura bitters

Shake well over ice and strain into an old fashioned glass.

Elk's Own Cocktail

1½ oz. rye
¾ oz. port
1 egg white, thoroughly beaten
1 tsp. powdered sugar
1 tbsp. lemon juice
Pineapple wedge

Shake well with ice and strain into a cocktail glass. Garnish with pineapple wedge.

El Presidente

1½ oz. light rum
½ oz. curaçao
½ oz. dry vermouth
1–2 dashes grenadine

Shake well with ice and strain into a cocktail glass.

Eye-Opener

2 oz. light rum
1 tsp. white crème de cacao
1 tsp. triple sec
1 tsp. Pernod
1 egg yolk, beaten
½ tsp. powdered sugar

Shake well with ice and strain into a sour glass.

Fino Martini

2 oz. gin
2 oz. fino sherry
Lemon peel

Stir gin and sherry with ice in mixing glass. Strain into a cocktail glass. Add twist of lemon.

Fish House Punch

Powdered sugar
3 cups lemon juice
1½ quarts brandy
1 pint peach brandy
1 pint rum

1 quart club soda
1 pint strong cold tea
  Fruits

Add powdered sugar to the lemon juice and pour over a block of ice in a punch bowl. Stir well. Add remaining ingredients, stir well, and garnish with seasonal fruits.

Flying Grasshopper

¾ oz. vodka
¾ oz. white crème de menthe
¾ oz. green crème de menthe

Stir well with ice and strain into a cocktail glass.

Flying Scotchman

1½ oz. scotch
1½ oz. sweet vermouth
  2 dashes bitters
¼ tsp. sugar syrup

Stir well with ice and strain into a cocktail glass.

Foghorn

2 oz. gin
1 tbsp. lime juice
  Ginger ale
  Lime slice

Pour gin and lime juice over ice into a highball glass. Fill glass with ginger ale, stir, and add lime slice.

Fox River

1½ oz. rye
½ oz. dark crème de cacao
1–2 dashes orange bitters
Lemon peel

Shake liquids well with ice and strain into a cocktail glass. Top with twist of lemon.

Frankenjack Cocktail

1 oz. gin
½ oz. apricot brandy
½ oz. triple sec
½ oz. dry vermouth
Maraschino cherry

Shake liquids well with ice and strain into an old fashioned glass. Garnish with cherry.

French 75

1½ oz. cognac
½ oz. sugar syrup
1 tbsp. lemon juice
Cold brut champagne
Lemon peel

Shake first three ingredients with ice. Pour into a highball glass and fill glass with champagne. Top with twist of lemon.

Frisco Sour

1½ oz. blended whiskey
¾ oz. Benedictine
1 tsp. lemon juice
1 tsp. lime juice
Orange slice

Shake liquids well with ice and strain into a sour glass. Garnish with orange slice.

Froth Blower Cocktail

---

2 oz. gin
1 tsp. grenadine
1 egg white, well beaten

Shake well with ice and pour into an old fashioned glass.

Froupe

1½ oz. brandy
1½ oz. sweet vermouth
   1 tsp. Benedictine

Stir with ice and strain into a cocktail glass.

Frozen Daiquiri

---

2 oz. light rum
½ oz. lime juice
1 tsp. sugar

Blend all ingredients at low speed with 1 cup of crushed ice until mixture is slushy. Pour into a saucer-shaped champagne glass.

Fuzzy Navel

---

3 oz. peach schnapps
3 oz. orange juice
   Orange slice

Pour schnapps and juice over ice into a collins glass. Garnish with orange slice.

General Harrison's Eggnog

1 cup dry white wine
1 egg
1 tsp. sugar

Blend well with crushed ice and pour into a highball glass.

Gibson

2½ oz. gin
1–2 dashes dry vermouth
    Cocktail onion

Stir with ice and strain into a cocktail glass. Garnish with cocktail onion.

Gilroy

1 oz. gin
1 oz. cherry brandy
½ oz. dry vermouth
½ oz. lemon juice
1–2 dashes orange bitters

Shake well with ice and pour into an old fashioned glass.

Gimlet

2 oz. gin
¼ oz. Rose's lime juice
    Lime slice

Shake well with ice and strain into an old fashioned glass. Garnish with lime slice.

Gin and Tonic

2 oz. gin
  Tonic water
  Lime wedge

Pour gin over ice into a collins glass. Fill glass with tonic. Squeeze lime wedge over the glass; then drop it in.

Gin Daisy

2 oz. gin
1 oz. lemon juice
1/4 oz. grenadine
1/2 tsp. sugar syrup
  Club soda
  Orange slice

Shake first four ingredients with ice and pour into a highball glass. Fill with club soda and garnish with orange slice.

Gin Fizz

2 oz. gin
1/2 oz. sugar syrup
1 1/2 tbsp. lemon juice
1 tbsp. lime juice
  Club soda
  Maraschino cherry

Shake first four ingredients with ice and pour into a highball glass. Fill glass with club soda and garnish with maraschino cherry.

Gin Rickey

2 oz. gin
  Club soda
1 tbsp. lime juice

Pour gin over ice in a highball glass. Fill glass with club soda. Add lime juice and stir.

Glogg

8 oz. raisins
1/4 oz. cardamom seeds
1/2 oz. whole cloves
   Orange peel
   Almonds
   Cinnamon sticks
2 quarts water
1 cup sugar
2 quarts port
1 pint brandy

Put the fruit and spices and sugar in a pan with the water and bring to a boil. Lower heat and simmer 45 minutes. Add port and brandy and bring to a boil again, briefly. May be served hot or cold.

Gloom Lifter

1 1/2 oz. blended whiskey
3/4 oz. brandy
1/2 oz. raspberry brandy
1 tsp. sugar syrup
1 tsp. lemon juice
1/2 egg white

Shake well with ice and pour into an old fashioned glass.

Gold Cadillac

2 oz. Galliano
1 oz. white crème de cacao
1 oz. heavy cream

Mix with crushed ice in blender until creamy. Strain into a cocktail glass.

Golden Dawn

2 oz. gin
¾ oz. apricot brandy
2 oz. orange juice
1 tbsp. lime juice
Dash grenadine

Shake well with ice and strain into a cocktail glass.

Golden Slipper

1 oz. apricot brandy
1 oz. yellow Chartreuse
1 egg yolk

Shake well with crushed ice and pour into a cocktail glass.

Grapefruit Cocktail

1½ oz. gin
1 oz. grapefruit juice
1 tsp. maraschino liqueur
Maraschino cherry

Shake well with ice. Strain into a chilled cocktail glass and top with cherry.

Grasshopper

1 oz. crème de menthe
1 oz. white crème de cacao
1 oz. light cream

Shake well with crushed ice and strain into a cocktail glass.

Green Dragon

1½ oz. gin
1 oz. green crème de menthe
½ oz. kümmel
½ oz. lemon juice
Dash orange bitters

Shake well with crushed ice and strain into a cocktail glass.

Grog

2 oz. rum
1 tbsp. lemon juice
1 tsp. sugar
5–6 cloves
Cinnamon stick
Boiling water
Lemon slice

Mix first five ingredients in a warm mug with boiling water. Stir to dissolve the sugar. Garnish with lemon slice.

Gypsy

2 oz. vodka
½ oz. Benedictine
1 tsp. lemon juice
1 tsp. orange juice
Orange slice

Shake liquids well with ice and strain into a cocktail glass. Garnish with orange slice.

Harvard

1½ oz. brandy
½ oz. sweet vermouth

48

¼ oz. lemon juice
1 tsp. grenadine
Dash Angostura bitters

Shake well with ice and strain into a cocktail glass.

Harvey Wallbanger

1½ oz. vodka
½ oz. Galliano
4 oz. orange juice

Stir vodka and orange juice with ice cubes in a collins glass.
Float Galliano on top.

Hasty Cocktail

1½ oz. gin
½ oz. dry vermouth
½ tsp. grenadine
1–2 dashes Pernod

Shake well with ice and strain into a cocktail glass.

Hawaiian

1½ oz. gin
1 oz. pineapple juice
½ egg white, beaten
1–2 dashes orange bitters

Shake well with ice and strain into an old fashioned glass.

Highball

1½ oz. whiskey
Club soda

Stir lightly with ice in a highball glass.

Hoffman House

1½ oz. gin
½ oz. dry vermouth
   Dash orange bitters
   Cocktail olive

Stir liquids with ice. Strain into a cocktail glass and add olive.

Honeymoon

1½ oz. apple brandy
¾ oz. Benedictine
1 oz. lemon juice
1–2 dashes curaçao

Shake well with cracked ice and pour into a cocktail glass.

Hop Toad

1 oz. light rum
1 oz. apricot brandy
1 oz. lime juice

Shake well with ice and strain into a cocktail glass.

Horse's Neck

1 lemon
2 oz. blended whiskey
   Dash Angostura bitters
   Ginger ale

Cut the peel from the lemon in a single spiral and drop the peel into a collins glass. Add ice, the whiskey, and the bitters. Fill glass with ginger ale and stir gently.

Hot Brick Toddy

1 tsp. sugar syrup
¼ tsp. ground cinnamon
1 tbsp. butter
   Boiling water
2 oz. blended, bourbon, Canadian, or rye whiskey

Warm a clear glass mug with hot water. Dissolve syrup, cinnamon, and butter in the mug in a little boiling water. Stir in whiskey; then fill mug with boiling water.

Hot Buttered Rum

½ tsp. sugar
   Boiling water
1½ oz. rum
2 cloves
1 tbsp. butter

Dissolve sugar in a little boiling water in a clear glass mug. Add rum and cloves. Fill mug with boiling water and stir. Float butter on top.

Hurricane

1 oz. light rum
1 oz. gold rum
½ oz. passion fruit syrup
½ oz. lime juice

Shake well with ice and strain into a cocktail glass.

Imperial

1½ oz. gin
1½ oz. dry vermouth
1–2 dashes maraschino liqueur
1–2 dashes Angostura bitters
Green olive

Shake or stir liquids with ice. Strain into a cocktail glass and add olive.

Irish Coffee

1 tsp. superfine sugar
Hot black coffee
1½ oz. Irish whiskey
2 tbsp. whipped cream

In a heavy goblet, a large wineglass, or a clear glass mug warmed by rinsing with hot water, dissolve the sugar in a little hot coffee. Add the whiskey. Fill mug with coffee and top with whipped cream.

Irish Shillelagh

1½ oz. Irish whiskey
½ oz. sloe gin
½ oz. light rum
1 oz. lemon juice
1 tsp. sugar syrup
2 peach slices, diced
Maraschino cherry
Fresh raspberries

Shake first six ingredients well with cracked ice and pour into an old fashioned glass. Garnish with cherry and raspberries.

Jack Rose

1 oz. apple brandy
2 tsp. grenadine

1 oz. lime juice
    Dash lemon juice

Shake well over ice and strain into a cocktail glass.

Jamaica Glow

1½ oz. gin
    ½ oz. dry red wine
    ¼ oz. dark Jamaican rum
    ½ oz. orange juice
    Lime slice

Shake liquids well with ice. Strain into a cocktail glass and garnish with lime slice.

Japanese

2 oz. brandy
    ¼ oz. orgeat syrup
    ¼ oz. lime juice
    Dash Angostura bitters
    Lime peel

Shake first four ingredients well with ice and strain into a cocktail glass. Top with twist of lime.

Japanese Fizz

2 oz. blended whiskey
    ¾ oz. port
    ½ oz. lemon juice
    1 tsp. sugar
    Club soda
    Orange peel
    Pineapple spear

Shake or blend first four ingredients with ice, and pour into a highball glass. Fill glass with soda and garnish with orange peel and pineapple.

Jewel

  1 oz. gin
  1 oz. sweet vermouth
  1 oz. green Chartreuse
  1–2 dashes orange bitters
  Lemon peel

Shake liquids well with ice and strain into an old fashioned glass.
Twist lemon peel over the glass and drop it in.

Jockey Club

  2 oz. gin
  ½ tsp. crème de noyaux
  ½ tsp. lemon juice
  1–2 dashes Angostura bitters
  1–2 dashes orange bitters

Shake well with ice and strain into an old fashioned glass.

Judge, Jr.

  1 oz. gin
  1 oz. light rum
  ½ oz. lemon juice
  1 tsp. grenadine

Shake well with ice and strain into a cocktail glass.

Knockout

  1 oz. gin
  1 oz. dry vermouth
  1 oz. Pernod
  Dash lemon juice
  Maraschino cherry

Shake liquids well with ice and strain into a cocktail glass. Top with maraschino cherry.

La Jolla

1½ oz. brandy
½ oz. crème de banane
¼ oz. lemon juice
1 tsp. orange juice

Shake well with ice and strain into a cocktail glass.

Ladies' Cocktail

1½ oz. blended whiskey
1 tsp. anisette
1–2 dashes Pernod
1–2 dashes Angostura bitters
Pineapple spear

Shake liquids well with ice and strain into an old fashioned glass. Garnish with pineapple.

Lawhill Cocktail

1½ oz. blended whiskey
½ oz. dry vermouth
¼ tsp. Pernod
¼ tsp. maraschino liqueur
½ oz. orange juice
Dash Angostura bitters

Shake well with ice and strain into a cocktail glass.

Leapfrog

1½ oz. gin
½ oz. lemon juice
    Ginger ale

Stir gin and lemon juice in a collins glass with ice. Fill glass with ginger ale.

Liberty

1½ oz. Calvados
¾ oz. light rum
    Maraschino cherry

Shake well with ice and strain into a cocktail glass. Garnish with cherry.

Little Devil

1 oz. gin
1 oz. gold rum
½ oz. triple sec
½ oz. lemon juice

Stir with crushed ice and strain into a cocktail glass.

Long Island Iced Tea

½ oz. vodka
½ oz. gin
½ oz. rum
½ oz. tequila
3 tbsp. lemon juice
    Cola
    Lemon slice

Mix first five ingredients with ice in a collins glass. Add cola and garnish with lemon slice.

Los Angeles Cocktail

1½ oz. blended whiskey
1 oz. lemon juice
1 tsp. sugar
1–2 dashes sweet vermouth
1 egg, beaten

Shake well with crushed ice and pour into an old fashioned glass.

Love

2 oz. sloe gin
½ egg white, beaten
½ oz. lemon juice
1–2 dashes grenadine

Shake well with crushed ice and pour into a cocktail glass.

Mai Tai

1 oz. Jamaican rum
1 oz. Martinique rum
½ oz. curaçao
¼ oz. sugar syrup
¼ oz. orgeat syrup
Mint sprig
Fresh fruit chunks

Shake liquids well with cracked ice and pour into an old fashioned glass. Top with a mint spring and assorted fruit on a spear.

Maiden's Blush

1½ oz. gin
1 tsp. curaçao
½ tsp. lemon juice
½ tsp. grenadine

Shake well with ice and pour into a sour glass.

Manhasset

1½ oz. blended whiskey
½ oz. lemon juice
¼ oz. sweet vermouth
¼ oz. dry vermouth
  Lemon peel

Shake liquids well with ice and strain into a cocktail glass. Top with twist of lemon.

Manhattan

1½ oz. blended whiskey
½ oz. sweet vermouth
1 or 2 dashes Angostura bitters
  Maraschino cherry

Shake liquids well over ice and strain into a cocktail glass. Garnish with a maraschino cherry.

Margarita

1½ oz. white or gold tequila
½ oz. triple sec
1½ tbsp. lime juice
  Coarse salt

Shake liquids well with cracked ice. Moisten the rim of a cocktail glass with some lime juice and dip it into coarse salt. Strain drink into frosted glass.

Martinez

1 oz. gin
4 oz. dry vermouth
  Dash bitters
2 dashes maraschino liqueur
  Lemon slice

Shake liquids with ice. Strain into a cocktail glass and garnish with lemon slice.

Martini

2 oz. gin
  Dry vermouth
  Green olive or lemon peel

Stir gin and vermouth with plenty of ice and strain into a cocktail glass. Garnish with olive or lemon twist. The amount of vermouth used depends on how dry you like your martini; add anything from a dash to an ounce or two depending on your taste.

Mary Pickford

1½ oz. light Martinique rum
¼ oz. maraschino liqueur
¼ oz. grenadine
1½ oz. pineapple juice

Shake well with crushed ice and pour into a cocktail glass.

Melon Cocktail

1½ oz. gin
½ oz. maraschino liqueur
½ oz. lemon juice
Maraschino cherry

Shake liquids well with ice. Strain into a cocktail glass and garnish with cherry.

Merry Widow

1 oz. gin
1 oz. dry vermouth
1–2 dashes Pernod
1–2 dashes Benedictine
1–2 dashes Angostura bitters
Lemon peel

Shake liquids well with ice. Strain into a cocktail glass. Twist lemon peel over glass; then drop it in.

Merry Widow No. 2

1½ oz. cherry brandy
1 oz. maraschino liqueur
Maraschino cherry

Shake well with ice and strain into a cocktail glass. Garnish with cherry.

Miami Beach Cocktail

1 oz. scotch

1 oz. dry vermouth
1 oz. grapefruit juice

Shake well with ice and strain into a cocktail glass.

Mikado

1½ oz. brandy
1–2 dashes curaçao
1–2 dashes crème de noyaux
1–2 dashes orgeat syrup
1–2 dashes Angostura bitters

Shake well with crushed ice and pour into a cocktail glass.

Mimosa

Champagne
Orange juice

Fill a chilled wineglass half with champagne, half with orange juice. Stir gently.

Mint Julep

15 mint leaves
1 tsp. sugar
3 oz. bourbon
6 oz. club soda

Combine about 12 mint leaves with the sugar. Add bourbon and soda; stir to dissolve sugar. Strain into a collins glass filled with crushed ice. Garnish with remaining mint.

Mocha Mint

¾ oz. Kahlúa
¾ oz. crème de menthe
¾ oz. crème de cacao

Shake well with ice and strain into a cocktail glass.

Modern

¾ oz. scotch
1½ oz. sloe gin
1–2 dashes Pernod
1–2 dashes grenadine
1–2 dashes orange bitters

Shake well with crushed ice and pour into an old fashioned glass.

Montana

2 oz. brandy
2 tsp. port
2 tsp. dry vermouth

Stir with ice in a cocktail glass.

Morning Cocktail

1 oz. brandy
1 oz. dry vermouth
1–2 dashes Pernod
1–2 dashes curaçao

1–2 dashes maraschino liqueur
1–2 dashes orange bitters

Shake well with crushed ice and pour into an old fashioned glass.

Morning Glory Fizz

2 oz. scotch
¼ oz. Pernod
½ oz. lemon juice
1 tsp. sugar
½ egg white
    Dash Peychaud's bitters
    Club soda
    Lemon slice

Shake or blend first six ingredients with crushed ice and pour into a collins glass. Fill glass with club soda and garnish with lemon slice.

Moscow Mule

2 oz. vodka
1 tsp. lime juice
    Ginger beer
    Lime slice

Mix vodka and lime juice in a clear glass mug or old fashioned glass with ice. Fill glass with ginger beer and garnish with lime slice.

Moulin Rouge

1½ oz. sloe gin
½ oz. sweet vermouth
1–2 dashes Angostura bitters

Shake well with crushed ice and pour into a cocktail glass.

Mulled Claret

2 oz. honey
1 cup water
1 750-milliliter bottle red wine
1 pint ruby port
1 cup brandy
6 whole cloves
3 broken cinnamon sticks
½ tsp. grated nutmeg
Lemon peel

Dissolve honey in water over low heat in a saucepan or chafing dish. Add remaining ingredients and heat, stirring, but do not bring to a boil.

Nevins Cocktail

1½ oz. bourbon
½ oz. apricot brandy
1 oz. grapefruit juice
1 tsp. lemon juice
1–2 dashes Angostura bitters

Shake well with ice and strain into an old fashioned glass.

New York

1½ oz. rye
½ oz. lime juice
1 tsp. sugar syrup
1–2 dashes grenadine
Orange peel

Shake liquids well with crushed ice and pour into an old fashioned glass. Top with twist of orange.

New York Sour

2 oz. blended whiskey
½ oz. lemon juice
1 tsp. sugar syrup
½ oz. dry red wine
Lemon slice

Shake or blend whiskey, juice, and syrup with crushed ice and pour into a sour glass. Add wine, stir, and garnish with lemon slice.

Old Fashioned

2 oz. American or Canadian whiskey
Dash sugar syrup
Dash Angostura bitters
Dash water

Stir in an old fashioned glass and add ice cubes.

Olympic

1 oz. brandy
1 oz. curaçao
1 oz. orange juice

Shake well with crushed ice and pour into a cocktail glass.

Opening Cocktail

1½ oz. Canadian whisky
1 tsp. sweet vermouth
1 tsp. grenadine

Stir with ice and strain into a cocktail glass.

Opera

1½ oz. gin
¾ oz. red Dubonnet
½ oz. maraschino liqueur
Orange peel

Shake liquids well with ice and strain into a cocktail glass. Twist orange peel over the glass; then drop it in.

Orange Blossom

1½ oz. gin
1 oz. lemon juice
Orange slice

Shake gin and juice well with ice and strain into a cocktail glass. Garnish with orange slice.

Paddy Cocktail

1½ oz. Irish whiskey
¾ oz. sweet vermouth
1–2 dashes Angostura bitters

Shake well with ice and strain into a cocktail glass.

Paisley Martini

2 oz. gin
½ tsp. dry vermouth
½ tsp. scotch

Shake or stir with ice and strain into a cocktail glass.

Paradise

2 oz. gin
1 oz. orange juice
1 oz. apricot brandy
Orange slice

Shake liquids well with ice and strain into a cocktail glass.
Garnish with orange slice.

Parisian

1 oz. gin
1 oz. dry vermouth
1 oz. crème de cassis

Stir with ice and strain into a cocktail glass.

Parisian Blonde

1 oz. dark Jamaican rum
1 oz. triple sec
1 oz. heavy cream

Shake well with ice and strain into a cocktail glass.

Park Avenue Cocktail

1½ oz. gin
½ oz. cherry brandy
½ oz. lime juice
¼ oz. maraschino liqueur

Stir well with ice and strain into a cocktail glass.

Peach Blow Fizz

    2 oz. gin
    1 oz. lemon juice
    1 oz. heavy cream
    1 tsp. sugar syrup
    4 strawberries, mashed
      Club soda

Shake or blend first five ingredients with ice. Pour into a highball glass; fill glass with club soda and stir.

Phoebe Snow

    1½ oz. cognac
    1½ oz. red Dubonnet
       Dash Pernod

Shake well with ice and strain into a cocktail glass.

Picon

    1 oz. Amer Picon
    1 oz. sweet vermouth

Shake well with cracked ice and pour into a cocktail glass.

Piña Colada

    2 oz. gold rum
    2 oz. cream of coconut
    4 oz. pineapple juice

Shake well with cracked ice and pour into a collins glass.

Pink Gin

2 oz. gin
1–2 dashes Angostura bitters

Stir with plenty of ice and strain into a cocktail glass.

Pink Lady

1½ oz. gin
1½ oz. applejack
1 oz. lemon juice
1 tsp. sugar syrup
1 tsp. grenadine
½ egg white, beaten

Shake well with cracked ice and strain into a cocktail glass.

Planter's Punch

1½ oz. dark rum
2 oz. orange juice
¾ oz. lemon juice
¼ tsp. grenadine
Orange slice
Maraschino cherry

Shake well with ice and strain into a collins glass. Garnish with orange slice and cherry.

Planter's Punch No. 2

2 oz. Puerto Rican rum
1 oz. dark Jamaican rum
½ oz. sugar syrup
1 oz. lime juice
1–2 dashes Angostura bitters

Club soda
Orange slices
Lime slices

Shake or blend first five ingredients with ice and pour into a collins glass. Fill glass with soda and garnish with orange and lime slices.

Poker Cocktail

1½ oz. rum
¾ oz. sweet vermouth
Orange peel

Shake rum and vermouth with ice and strain into a chilled cocktail glass. Top with twist of orange.

Polonaise

1½ oz. brandy
½ oz. dry sherry
½ oz. blackberry brandy
Dash lemon juice

Shake or blend with crushed ice and strain into an old fashioned glass over ice cubes.

Poop Deck

1 oz. brandy
½ oz. blackberry brandy
½ oz. port

Shake well with ice and strain into a cocktail glass.

Preakness

1½ oz. blended whiskey
¼ oz. sweet vermouth
¼ oz. Benedictine
   Dash Angostura bitters

Shake well with ice and strain into a cocktail glass.

Princeton

1½ oz. gin
½ oz. port
2 dashes orange bitters

Shake well with cracked ice and strain into a cocktail glass.

Quarterdeck

1½ oz. dark rum
½ oz. cream sherry
1 tsp. lime juice

Shake well with ice and strain into an old fashioned glass. Add ice.

Quebec Cocktail

1½ oz. Canadian whisky
½ oz. dry vermouth
½ oz. Amer Picon
1 tsp. maraschino liqueur

Shake well with ice and strain into a highball glass. Add ice.

Racquet Club

1½ oz. gin
½ oz. dry vermouth
Dash orange bitters

Shake well with ice and strain into a cocktail glass.

Ramos Gin Fizz

2 oz. gin
½ oz. lime juice
½ oz. lemon juice
2 tsp. sugar
1 egg white, beaten
2 tsp. heavy cream
1–2 dashes orange flower water
Club soda

Shake all ingredients except club soda with ice and strain into a collins glass. Fill glass with soda.

Rattlesnake

1½ oz. blended whiskey
1 tsp. lemon juice
1 tsp. sugar syrup
1 egg white, beaten
1–2 dashes Pernod

Shake well with cracked ice and strain into an old fashioned glass. Add ice.

Red Cloud

1½ oz. gin
½ oz. apricot brandy

¹/₂ oz. lemon juice
1 tsp. grenadine
Dash Angostura bitters

Shake well with ice and strain into an old fashioned glass. Add ice.

Remsen Cooler

2¹/₂ oz. scotch
1 tsp. sugar syrup
Club soda
Lemon peel

Combine scotch and sugar syrup with ice in a highball glass. Fill glass with club soda and stir. Top with a lemon twist. (For Gin Remsen Cooler, substitute gin for scotch, and ginger ale for club soda.)

Rob Roy

1¹/₂ oz. scotch
¹/₂ oz. sweet vermouth
Dash Angostura bitters

Shake well over ice and strain into a cocktail glass.

Rock and Rye Cooler

1 oz. rock and rye
1 oz. vodka
¹/₂ oz. lime juice
Lemon-lime soda

Shake first three ingredients with ice. Strain into a highball glass, add ice, and fill glass with lemon-lime soda.

Rolls-Royce

1½ oz. gin
½ oz. sweet vermouth
½ oz. dry vermouth
1–2 dashes Benedictine

Shake well with ice and strain into a cocktail glass.

Royal Gin Fizz

2½ oz. gin
2 tbsp. lemon juice
2½ tsp. sugar syrup
1 egg
Club soda

Shake first four ingredients with ice and strain into a collins glass. Add ice and fill glass with club soda.

Royal Smile

1½ oz. gin
1½ oz. grenadine
Dash lemon juice

Shake well with ice and strain into a cocktail glass.

Ruby Fizz

3 oz. sloe gin

1 oz. lemon juice
1 tsp. sugar syrup
1 tsp. grenadine
1 egg white
  Club soda

Shake first five ingredients with ice and strain into a highball glass. Fill glass with club soda.

Rum and Coke

2 oz. rum
  Cola
  Lime wedge

Pour rum over ice in a collins glass and fill glass with cola. Squeeze lime wedge over the glass; then drop it in.

Rum Martini

2 oz. light rum
½ oz. dry vermouth

Stir well with ice cubes and strain into a cocktail glass.

Rum Screwdriver

1½ oz. light rum
4–6 oz. orange juice

Pour rum over ice in a highball glass. Fill glass with orange juice and stir well.

Rum Sour

2 oz. rum
½ oz. lemon juice
1 tsp. orange juice
1 tsp. sugar syrup
Lemon peel

Shake well with ice and strain into a sour glass. Add lemon twist.

Russian Bear

1½ oz. vodka
½ oz. crème de cacao
½ oz. heavy cream

Shake well with ice and strain into a cocktail glass.

Russian Cocktail

1 oz. gin
1 oz. vodka
½ oz. white crème de cacao

Shake well with ice and strain into a cocktail glass.

Rusty Nail

1 oz. scotch
1 oz. Drambuie

Pour ingredients over ice in an old fashioned glass and stir.

Moisten the rim of an old fashioned glass and dip it in salt. Add ice, pour in vodka, and fill glass with grapefruit juice. Stir well.

San Francisco

1 oz. sloe gin
½ oz. dry vermouth
½ oz. sweet vermouth
2 dashes Angostura bitters
2 dashes orange bitters

Shake well with ice and strain into a cocktail glass.

Sangria

1 750-milliliter bottle dry red wine
3 oz. brandy
1 oz. curaçao
3 oz. lemon juice
3 oz. orange juice
2 oz. sugar
Orange slices
Lemon slices

Stir well with ice in a large pitcher and serve in large wineglasses. Garnish with orange and lemon slices.

Saratoga

2 oz. brandy
1 oz. pineapple juice
1–2 dashes Angostura bitters
1–2 dashes maraschino liqueur

Shake well with ice and strain into a cocktail glass.

Scotch Cooler

3 oz. scotch
1–2 dashes white crème de menthe
Club soda

Combine scotch and crème de menthe in a collins glass and stir. Add ice, fill glass with club soda, and stir again.

Scotch Holiday Sour

2 oz. scotch
1 oz. cherry brandy
1 oz. lemon juice
1 oz. sweet vermouth
1/2 egg white, beaten
Lemon peel

Shake first five ingredients with ice and strain into a sour glass. Add twist of lemon.

Scotch Mist

2 oz. scotch
Lemon peel

Fill an old fashioned glass with cracked ice. Pour scotch over ice. Twist lemon peel over the glass, and drop peel in glass.

Scotch Sour

2 oz. scotch
1/2 oz. lemon juice
1 tsp. sugar syrup
Maraschino cherry
Orange peel

Shake first three ingredients with ice and strain into a sour glass. Top with maraschino cherry and twist of orange.

Screwdriver

1½ oz. vodka
    Orange juice

Pour vodka into an old fashioned glass over ice. Fill glass with orange juice.

September Morn

  2 oz. light rum
½ oz. lime juice
  1 tsp. grenadine
½ egg white

Shake well with ice and strain into a cocktail glass.

Seven and Seven

1½ oz. blended whiskey
    Lemon-lime soda

Pour whiskey over ice in an old fashioned glass, fill with soda and stir gently.

Sevilla

1 oz. light rum
1 oz. sweet vermouth
  Orange peel

Shake well with ice and strain into an old fashioned glass. Add ice and twist of orange.

Shamrock

1 oz. Irish whiskey
1 oz. dry vermouth
3–4 drops green crème de menthe
3–4 drops green Chartreuse

Shake well with ice and strain into a cocktail glass.

Shanghai

1½ oz. light rum
½ oz. lemon juice
1 oz. anisette
2–3 dashes grenadine

Shake well with ice and strain into a highball glass. Add ice.

Sherry Cobbler

3 oz. sherry
½ oz. orange juice
1 tsp. powdered sugar
1 mint sprig

Stir sherry, juice, and sugar in an old fashioned glass. Add ice and mint.

Sherry Twist

1½ oz. sherry
½ oz. dry vermouth
½ oz. brandy
2–3 dashes triple sec
2–3 dashes lemon juice
Cinnamon stick

Combine liquid ingredients with ice and shake well. Strain into a collins glass. Add ice and cinnamon stick.

Sidecar

2 oz. brandy
½ oz. curaçao
½ oz. lemon juice

Shake well with ice and strain into an old fashioned glass. Add ice.

Silver Bullet

1½ oz. gin
1 oz. kümmel
1 oz. lemon juice

Shake well over ice and strain into a cocktail glass.

Singapore Sling

2 oz. gin
1 oz. cherry brandy
2 dashes Angostura bitters
1 oz. lemon juice
Club soda
2 dashes Benedictine

Shake first four ingredients with ice and strain into a collins glass. Add ice. Fill glass with club soda and stir. Float Benedictine on top.

Sir Walter Raleigh

1½ oz. brandy
½ oz. light rum
1 tsp. curaçao
1 tsp. lime juice
1 tsp. grenadine

Shake well with ice and strain into an old fashioned glass. Add ice.

Sloe Gin Fizz

1 oz. sloe gin
1 oz. gin
½ oz. lemon juice
Club soda

Shake first three ingredients with ice and strain into a highball glass. Add ice. Fill glass with club soda.

Snowball

1 oz. gin
1 tsp. white crème de menthe
1 tsp. heavy cream
1 tsp. anisette
1 tsp. crème de violette

Shake well with ice and strain into a cocktail glass.

Soul Kiss

1 oz. Dubonnet
1 oz. orange juice
1 oz. sweet vermouth
1 oz. dry vermouth

Shake well with ice and strain into a cocktail glass. Add ice.

Soviet Cocktail

2 oz. vodka
½ oz. dry vermouth
½ oz. amontillado
Lemon peel

Shake well with ice and strain into a cocktail glass. Add ice and a twist of lemon.

Special Rough

1½ oz. apple brandy
1½ oz. brandy
2–3 dashes Pernod

Shake well with ice and strain into a brandy glass. Add ice

Spritzer

5 oz. chilled Rhine wine
Chilled club soda
Lemon peel

Pour wine into a large goblet over ice and fill glass with soda. Garnish with lemon peel or fruit slices.

Star Daisy

1 oz. gin
1 oz. apple brandy
1 oz. lemon juice
1 tsp. sugar syrup
1 tsp. grenadine

Shake well with ice and strain into a cocktail glass.

Stinger

2 oz. brandy
1 oz. white crème de menthe

Shake well with ice and strain into a cocktail glass.

Stone Fence

2½ oz. apple brandy
2 dashes Angostura bitters
Sweet apple cider

Stir brandy and bitters with ice in an old fashioned glass. Fill glass with cider and stir.

Straight Law Cocktail

2½ oz. dry sherry
½ oz. gin
Lemon peel

Shake well with ice and strain into a cocktail glass. Add a twist of lemon.

Strawberry Daiquiri

1½ oz. rum
½ oz. strawberry schnapps
6 strawberries
1 oz. lime juice
1 tsp. powdered sugar

Shake well with ice and strain into a cocktail glass.

Strawberry Margarita

Lime rind
Coarse salt
1 oz. tequila
½ oz. triple sec
½ oz. strawberry schnapps
1 oz. lime juice
6 strawberries

Rub rim of cocktail glass with lime rind and dip rim in coarse salt. Shake liquids with ice and strain into glass. Garnish with strawberries.

Suissesse

1½ oz. Pernod
½ oz. anisette
1 egg white, beaten
Heavy cream (optional)

Shake first three ingredients with ice. Strain into an old fashioned glass filled with ice. Add a few drops of cream.

Tahiti Club

---

2 oz. gold rum
½ oz. lime juice
½ oz. lemon juice
½ oz. pineapple juice
½ oz. maraschino liqueur
Orange slice

Shake liquids well with ice. Strain into a cocktail glass. Add ice and orange slice.

Tango

1½ oz. gin
½ oz. dry vermouth
½ oz. sweet vermouth
1 oz. orange juice
Dash curaçao

Shake well with ice and strain into an old fashioned glass. Add ice.

Temptation Cocktail

1½ oz. blended whiskey
½ oz. Dubonnet
3 or 4 drops Pernod
3 or 4 drops curaçao
Lemon peel
Orange peel

Shake liquids well with ice and strain into a cocktail glass. Add ice and twists of lemon and orange.

Tempter Cocktail

1½ oz. port
1½ oz. apricot brandy

Shake well with ice and strain into an old fashioned glass. Add ice.

Tequila Manhattan

1½ oz. gold tequila
½ oz. sweet vermouth
Lime peel

Shake liquids well with ice and strain into a cocktail glass. Add ice and twist of lime.

Tequila Old Fashioned

1½ oz. gold tequila
1 tbsp. sugar syrup
2 dashes Angostura bitters
Dash club soda
Lemon peel
Pineapple spear

Stir tequila, sugar syrup, and bitters with ice in an old fashioned glass. Add soda, twist of lemon, and pineapple spear.

Tequila Sour

1½ oz. tequila
1 oz. lemon juice
1½ tsp. sugar syrup

Shake well with ice and strain into a sour glass.

Tequila Sunrise

2 oz. tequila
2 tsp. grenadine
½ oz. lime juice
Orange juice

Pour tequila, lime juice, and grenadine into a highball glass over ice. Fill glass with orange juice and stir. (For a Tijuana Sunrise, use 2 dashes of Angostura bitters instead of the grenadine.)

Tequini

2½ oz. tequila
½ oz. dry vermouth
Lemon twist or cocktail olive

Stir liquids with ice. Strain into a cocktail glass and add lemon twist or olive.

Third Degree

1½ oz. gin
½ oz. dry vermouth
1 tsp. Pernod

Shake well with ice and strain into a cocktail glass.

Third Rail

2 oz. dry vermouth
3 drops curaçao
Several drops white crème de menthe
Lemon peel

Shake liquids with ice and strain into an old fashioned glass. Add ice and twist of lemon.

Tom Collins

2 oz. gin
1½ oz. lemon juice
1½ tsp. sugar syrup
Club soda
Maraschino cherry

Combine first three ingredients in a collins glass and stir well. Add ice, fill glass with soda, and add cherry. (A John Collins uses ginger ale instead of club soda.)

Toreador

1½ oz. tequila
½ oz. white crème de cacao
Whipped cream
Cocoa powder

Shake tequila and crème de cacao with ice and strain into a sour glass. Add ice. Top with whipped cream and sprinkle with cocoa.

Torridora Cocktail

1½ oz. white rum
2 tsp. Tia Maria
1 tsp. heavy cream
1 tsp. 151-proof rum

Combine first three ingredients with ice and shake well. Strain into an old fashioned glass and add ice. Float the 151-proof rum on top.

Trois Rivières

1½ oz. Canadian whisky
½ oz. Dubonnet
½ tsp. triple sec
Lemon peel

Shake liquids with ice and strain into an old fashioned glass. Add ice and twist of lemon.

Tropical Cocktail

2½ oz. gin
1 oz. frozen pineapple juice concentrate
1 oz. guava nectar
Orange peel

Shake liquids with ice and strain into an old fashioned glass. Add ice and twist of orange.

Tulip

---

1 oz. apple brandy
½ oz. sweet vermouth
½ oz. lemon juice
½ oz. apricot brandy

Shake well with ice and strain into a cocktail glass.

Tuxedo

---

3 oz. sherry
½ oz. anisette
2 drops maraschino liqueur
2 dashes Angostura bitters

Shake well with ice and strain into a cocktail glass.

Ulanda

1½ oz. gin
½ oz. triple sec
Dash Pernod

Shake well with ice and strain into an old fashioned glass over ice.

Valencia

2 oz. apricot brandy
1 oz. orange juice
2 dashes orange bitters

Shake well with ice and strain into an old fashioned glass over ice.

Velvet Hammer

1 oz. triple sec
1 oz. white crème de cacao
1 oz. heavy cream

Shake well with ice and strain into a cocktail glass.

Vermouth Cassis

1½ oz. dry vermouth
½ oz. crème de cassis
Club soda
Lemon peel

Stir vermouth and cassis in a highball glass with ice. Fill glass with club soda and add twist of lemon.

Victor Cocktail

2 oz. sweet vermouth
1 oz. gin
1 oz. brandy

Shake well with ice. Strain into an old fashioned glass and add ice.

Vodka and Tonic

2 oz. vodka
   Tonic water
   Lime wedge

Pour vodka over ice in a collins glass and fill glass with tonic. Squeeze lime wedge over the glass and drop it in.

Vodka Gimlet

1½ oz. vodka
  1 oz. lime juice
1½ tsp. sugar syrup

Shake well with ice and strain into an old fashioned glass. Add ice.

Vodka Grasshopper

¾ oz. white crème de menthe
¾ oz. green crème de menthe
½ oz. vodka

Shake well with ice and strain into a cocktail glass.

Vodka Sling

2 oz. vodka
1½ tsp. Benedictine
1½ tsp. cherry brandy
1 tsp. lemon juice
Dash Angostura bitters
Dash orange bitters
Club soda

Shake first six ingredients with ice. Strain into a highball glass, add ice, and fill glass with club soda.

Vodka Stinger

1½ oz. vodka
1 oz. white crème de menthe

Shake well with ice. Strain into an old fashioned glass with ice.

Warsaw

1½ oz. vodka
½ oz. dry vermouth
½ oz. blackberry brandy
1 tsp. lemon juice
Lemon peel

Shake liquids well with ice and strain into an old fashioned glass. Add ice and twist of lemon.

Washington

1 oz. dry vermouth
1 oz. brandy
½ tsp. sugar syrup
1–2 dashes Angostura bitters

Shake well with ice and strain into a cocktail glass.

Waterbury

2½ oz. brandy
½ oz. lemon juice
1 tsp. sugar syrup
1 egg white, beaten
Several drops grenadine

Shake well with ice and strain into an old fashioned glass. Add ice.

Wedding Belle

1 oz. gin
1 oz. Dubonnet
½ oz. cherry brandy
1 oz. orange juice

Shake well with ice. Strain into a cocktail glass.

Weep No More

1½ oz. Dubonnet
1½ oz. brandy
1½ oz. lime juice
Several drops maraschino liqueur

Shake well with ice and strain into an old fashioned glass. Add ice.

Whiskey Cobbler

2½ oz. blended whiskey
½ oz. lemon juice
½ oz. grapefruit juice
½ oz. amaretto
Mint sprig

Combine all ingredients except mint in an old fashioned glass and stir well. Add ice and mint sprig.

Whiskey Daisy

1½ oz. blended whiskey
½ oz. lemon juice
½ oz. grenadine
Several drops triple sec
Club soda

Combine all ingredients except soda and shake well with ice. Strain into a collins glass, add ice, and fill glass with soda.

Whiskey Sour

2 oz. blended whiskey
½ oz. lemon juice
1 tbsp. sugar
Cherry slices
Orange slices

Shake well over ice and strain into a sour glass. Garnish with cherry and orange slices.

White Lily

1 oz. gin
1 oz. white rum
1 oz. triple sec
Several drops Pernod

Shake well with ice and strain into an old fashioned glass. Add ice.

White Lion

1½ oz. rum
1½ oz. lemon juice

1½ tsp. sugar syrup
   Several drops raspberry syrup
1–2 dashes Angostura bitters

Shake well with ice and strain into a cocktail glass.

White Rose

1½ oz. gin
½ oz. lime juice
½ oz. maraschino liqueur
1 tsp. sugar syrup
½ egg white
   Orange juice

Combine all ingredients except the orange juice, shake well with ice, and strain into an old fashioned glass. Add ice and fill glass with orange juice.

White Russian

1½ oz. vodka
¾ oz. Kahlúa
¾ oz. light cream

Fill an old fashioned glass with ice, add vodka and Kahlúa, then float the cream on top.

White Way

1 oz. brandy
1 oz. Pernod
1 oz. anisette

Shake well with ice and strain into an old fashioned glass. Add ice.

Widow's Kiss

1 oz. apple brandy
1/2 oz. Benedictine
1/2 oz. yellow Chartreuse
2 dashes Angostura bitters
1 strawberry

Shake liquid ingredients with ice and strain into an old fashioned glass. Add ice and strawberry.

Xanthia

1 oz. gin
1 oz. cherry brandy
1/2 oz. yellow Chartreuse

Shake well with ice and strain into an old fashioned glass. Add ice.

Yellow Parrot

1 oz. apricot brandy
1 oz. Pernod
1/2 oz. yellow Chartreuse

Shake well with ice and strain into an old fashioned glass. Add ice.

Zombie

2 oz. light rum
1 oz. lemon juice
1 oz. orange juice
1 oz. dark rum
1 oz. pineapple juice
1/2 oz. papaya juice
1/2 oz. grenadine

½ oz. sugar syrup
1 pineapple spear
1 mint sprig
½ oz. 151-proof rum
  Sugar

Combine all ingredients except pineapple, mint, 151-proof rum, and sugar, and shake well with ice. Strain into a collins glass and add ice. Add pineapple and mint. Float the 151-proof rum on top, and sprinkle with sugar.

8. Cautionary Wisdom

Today as a host you face a growing list of sensitive issues that can arise at any party, especially when the guests are people you don't know very well. There are three possibilities for which you should plan ahead: abstinence, overindulgence, and smoking.

Abstinence:

More people are deciding to limit or eliminate their use of alcohol, perhaps because they have recognized a problem, because of diet or other health considerations, or because they want to be able to drive safely. The considerate host will never try to talk a guest into having an alcoholic drink and will always provide plenty of attractive nonalcoholic alternatives—sparkling cider, for example, when champagne is being served, or some of the nonalcoholic drink recipes in the next chapter.

Overindulgence:

If you notice guests becoming intoxicated, make every effort to stop them from drinking anything more. Make sure they stay long enough to sober up, or see that they have an alternative way to get home. Do not let them drive while intoxicated.

To monitor the potential for intoxication of your guests—and for your own information when you may need to drive after having a drink away from home—the U.S. Department of Transportation gives the following guidelines for driving under the influence.

The chart gives the number of drinks a person may have over a two-hour period. One drink equals 12 oz. of beer, 4 oz. of wine, or 1½ oz. of 80-proof liquor. To use the chart, find your approximate body weight, then the number of drinks in each of three categories.

Body Weight	Be Careful After	Some Influence After	Don't Drive After
100	1 drink	2 drinks	3 drinks
120	1–2 drinks	2–3 drinks	3 drinks
140	2 drinks	3 drinks	4 drinks
160	2–3 drinks	3–4 drinks	4–5 drinks
180	3 drinks	4 drinks	5 drinks
200	3 drinks	4–5 drinks	5–6 drinks
220	3–4 drinks	4–6 drinks	6 drinks
240	4 drinks	4–6 drinks	6–7 drinks

It is always a good idea to have a designated driver who will refrain from drinking and who will be responsible for getting those who have been drinking home safely. This driver may be one half of a couple or one member of a group. If there is no designated driver, play it safe and call a taxi. Penalties for driving while intoxicated are becoming much stiffer, but even more important is the possibility of seriously injuring yourself, your companions, or other innocent people should you be involved in an accident.

Smoking:

If your home is generally a no smoking area, plan ahead for the smoking issue. Be sure to have ashtrays available to accommodate those guests who may smoke. If you don't plan to allow smoking in your home, perhaps you can invite guests to smoke on the patio. If you are quite strong in your anti-smoking position you may want to mention it to guests whom you don't know very well, in order to avoid embarrassing scenes after your party has gotten under way.

9. Alcohol-Free Drinks

Angostura Cocktail

---

1 tsp. Angostura bitters
Ginger ale

Stir well over ice in a highball glass.

Cajun Tomato

---

8 oz. tomato juice
1 tsp. lime juice
Dash garlic powder
Dash Tabasco sauce
Salt and pepper

Shake well over ice and strain into a cocktail glass.

Fizzy Lemonade

Juice of one lemon
2 tsp. powdered sugar
Sparkling water
Lemon slice
Lime slice

Combine lemon juice and sugar. Add ice and sparkling water. Garnish with lemon and lime.

Hot Tomato

8 oz. tomato juice
1 chili pepper, peeled
Dash lemon juice

Blend ingredients at high speed until mixture is smooth. Pour over ice into an old fashioned glass.

Lime and Coke

2 tbsp. lime juice
Cola
Lime slice

Combine lime juice and cola in a collins glass filled with ice. Garnish with lime slice.

No Rum Rickey

1 oz. lime juice
½ tsp. bitters
½ tsp. grenadine
Club soda
Lime peel

Combine first three ingredients with ice in an old fashioned glass. Fill glass with club soda and stir well. Garnish with twist of lime.

Orange and Tonic

5 oz. orange juice
5 oz. tonic water
   Orange slice

Pour ingredients over ice into a collins glass and stir. Garnish with orange slice.

Orange Cooler

Juice of two oranges
Powdered sugar
Sparkling water
Orange slice
Maraschino cherry

Combine orange juice and sugar with ice in a collins glass. Fill glass with sparkling water and garnish with orange slice and cherry.

Piña Non Colada

2 oz. pineapple juice
2 oz. cream of coconut
1 tbsp. lime juice
1 cup crushed ice
   Pineapple wedge

Blend ingredients until smooth. Pour into a collins glass. Garnish with pineapple wedge.

Shirley Temple

Dash grenadine
Ginger ale
Orange slice
Maraschino cherry

Add grenadine to collins glass over ice. Fill glass with ginger ale. Garnish with orange slice and cherry.

Tomato and Tonic

6 oz. tomato juice
3 oz. tonic water
Lemon or lime slice

Pour juice and tonic over ice into a collins glass. Garnish with lemon or lime slice.

Tomato Mexicano

6 oz. tomato juice
$\frac{1}{4}$ avocado, peeled, pitted, and sliced thin
$\frac{1}{4}$ chili pepper, peeled
Dash chili powder
Salt and pepper

Blend all ingredients at high speed until smooth. Pour over ice into a collins glass.

Unfuzzy Navel

3 oz. orange juice
3 oz. peach nectar
1 tbsp. lemon juice
1–2 dashes grenadine
Orange slice

Shake liquids with ice and strain into a collins glass. Garnish with orange slice.

Virgin Mary

    5 oz. tomato juice
    1 tsp. lemon juice
  1/2 tsp. Worcestershire sauce
    2 dashes Tabasco sauce
      Salt and pepper
      Lime slice

Pour tomato juice into a collins glass filled with ice. Stir in remaining liquid ingredients, and garnish with lime.

Glossary

Amaretto: An almond-flavored liqueur derived from apricot pits and spices.
Amer Picon: An orange-flavored liqueur.
Amontillado: A medium dry sherry.
Anisette: A liqueur flavored with aniseed.
Aperitif: A before-dinner drink.
Applejack: An apple brandy.

Benedictine: A liqueur flavored with herbs.
Bitters: Concentrated flavorings made from fruits and other natural ingredients.
Brandy: Fermented wine. The most common brandy is distilled from grape wine, but many other fruit wines are also distilled into brandy.

Calvados: An apple brandy distilled from hard cider, similar to applejack.
Campari: A bitter aperitif.
Chartreuse: An herb-flavored liqueur. Green Chartreuse is stronger; the yellow variety is sweeter.
Cognac: A brandy distilled from champagne.
Crème de banane: A banana-flavored liqueur.

Crème de cacao: A sweet chocolate-flavored liqueur made from cacao and vanilla beans.
Crème de cassis: A liqueur flavored with black currants.
Crème de menthe: A liqueur with peppermint and other mint flavorings.
Crème de noyaux: An almond-flavored liqueur.
Crème de violette: A liqueur flavored with violet petals.
Curaçao: A liqueur flavored with oranges and orange peel.

Drambuie: A liqueur made from scotch, honey, and herbs.
Dubonnet: An aperitif made from wine, available in red and white varieties.

Fino: A dry sherry.

Galliano: An herb-flavored Italian liqueur.
Gin: A mixture of spirits and flavoring agents, primarily juniper berries. London or dry gins are lighter than Holland or Geneva gins.
Grenadine: A pomegranate-flavored syrup.

Irish Cream: A liqueur made with Irish whiskey and cream.

Kirsch: A brandy distilled from cherries.
Kümmel: A liqueur flavored with caraway seeds.

Liqueur: A liqueur, or cordial, is a distilled, flavored spirit with at least 2½ percent sugar. Some of the more popular generic liqueurs are amaretto, triple sec, crème de cacao, and crème de menthe.

Maraschino liqueur: An Italian cherry liqueur.

Orgeat syrup: A syrup made from ground almonds and orange water.

Peppermint schnapps: A mint-flavored liqueur, not as sweet as crème de menthe.
Pernod: A brand of anise-flavored liqueur.
Port: A sweet wine fortified with brandy.

Rock and rye: A flavored rye whiskey liqueur.
Rose's lime juice: A sweet lime juice syrup.

Rum: Rum is distilled from sugarcane or molasses and may be lighter or darker depending on the method of distilling and aging. Caramel may be added to darken the color.

Sambuca: Liqueur with an anise-like flavor.
Sherry: A Spanish wine fortified with brandy.
Sloe gin: A liqueur flavored with the sloe berry, a wild plum.
Sugar syrup: A syrup made from sugar and water. Can be made by boiling a pint of water with a pound of sugar until sugar is fully dissolved.

Tequila: A Mexican liquor distilled from the juice of the blue agave plant. It is clear when it comes from the still. The golden color of some tequilas comes from aging in oak barrels or by adding caramel, or both.
Triple sec: An orange-flavored liqueur, which is not as sweet as curaçao.

Vermouth: An herb-flavored wine.
Vodka: A liquor distilled from grain, then often filtered through charcoal to remove any distinctive aroma or color. Some popular imported vodkas are flavored with lemon, pepper, or other flavoring agents.

Measurement Conversions

Ounce Equivalents (Liquid)

1 cup = 8 ounces
1 dash = $1/36$ ounce
1 jigger = $1\frac{1}{2}$ ounce
1 teaspoon = $1/6$ ounce
1 tablespoon = $1/2$ ounce

Miscellaneous

1 barrel (beer) = 31 gallons
$1/2$ barrel (beer) = 15.5 gallons
$1/2$ barrel (beer) = 1 keg of beer
1 dash = 6 drops
1 medium lemon = 3 tablespoons juice
1 medium orange = $1/3$ cup juice

Metric Bottle Sizes

4 liters = 135.2 ounces
3 liters = 101.4 ounces
1.75 liters = 59.2 ounces
1.5 liters = 50.7 ounces
1 liter = 33.8 ounces
750 milliliters = 25.4 ounces
375 milliliters = 12.7 ounces
200 milliliters = 6.8 ounces
167 milliliters = 6.3 ounces
100 milliliters = 3.4 ounces
 50 milliliters = 1.7 ounces

Index of Drinks Listed by Main Ingredient

Anisette
Baltimore Bracer, 18
Blanche, 22

Applejack
A.J., 16
Applejack Punch, 17
Barton Special, 20
Deauville Cocktail, 36
Dempsey Cocktail, 36
Pink Lady, 69

Benedictine
B&B, 18
Frisco Sour, 42–43

Bourbon
Brighton Punch, 28
Chapel Hill, 33
Mint Julep, 61
Nevins Cocktail, 64

Brandy
American Beauty, 16–17
B&B, 18
Baltimore Bracer, 18
Baltimore Eggnog, 19
Betsy Ross, 20
Between the Sheets, 21
Blackjack, 22
Bombay, 24
Bombay Punch, 24
Brandy Alexander, 24
Brandy Crusta, 24–25
Brandy Daisy, 25
Brandy Eggnog, 25
Brandy Fix, 26
Brandy Fizz, 26
Brandy Milk Punch, 26
Brandy Punch, 26–27
Brandy Sangaree, 27
Brandy Sour, 27
Brighton Punch, 28
Bull's Milk, 29

Cardinal Punch, 31
Carrol, 31
Champagne Cup, 32
Champagne Punch, 32
Cherry Blossom, 33
Classic Cocktail, 34–35
Coffee Flip, 35
Cold Deck, 35
Deauville Cocktail, 36
Depth Bomb, 36
Eggnog, 39
Fish House Punch, 40–41
Froupe, 43
Glogg, 46
Gloom Lifter, 46
Harvard, 48–49
Japanese, 53
La Jolla, 55
Mikado, 61
Montana, 62
Morning Cocktail, 62–63
Olympic, 65
Polonaise, 70
Poop Deck, 70
Sangria, 77
Saratoga, 77
Sidecar, 81
Sir Walter Raleigh, 81
Special Rough, 83
Stinger, 83
Victor Cocktail, 91
Washington, 92
Waterbury, 93
Weep No More, 93
White Way, 95

Brandies: Apple brandy
Apple Brandy Cocktail, 17
Bolero, 23
Depth Bomb, 36
Honeymoon, 50
Jack Rose, 52–53

Special Rough, 83
Star Daisy, 83
Stone Fence, 84
Tulip, 89
Widow's Kiss, 96

Apricot brandy
Apricot Lady, 18
Golden Slipper, 47
Hop Toad, 50
Paradise, 67
Tempter Cocktail, 86
Tulip, 89
Valencia, 90
Yellow Parrot, 96

Cherry brandy
Blood and Sand, 22
Cherry Blossom, 33
Gilroy, 44
Merry Widow No. 2, 60
Singapore Sling, 81
Xanthia, 96

Coffee brandy
Black Russian, 21
Cara Sposa, 31

Peach brandy
Fish House Punch, 40–41

Champagne
Black Velvet, 21
Buck's Fizz, 29
Champagne Cocktail, 32
Champagne Cup, 32
Champagne Punch, 32
Mimosa, 61

Cognac
French 75, 42
Phoebe Snow, 68

Crème de Banane
Banshee, 19
Capri, 30
La Jolla, 55

Crème de Cacao
Banshee, 19
Barbary Coast, 19
Brandy Alexander, 24
Capri, 30
Fox River, 42
Gold Cadillac, 46
Grasshopper, 47
Mocha Mint, 62
Toreador, 88
Velvet Hammer, 90

Crème de Menthe
Grasshopper, 47
Green Dragon, 48
Mocha Mint, 62
Vodka Grasshopper, 91
Vodka Stinger, 92

Dubonnet
Alfonso Cocktail, 16
Chocolate Soldier, 34
Dubonnet Cocktail, 38
Dubonnet Fizz, 38
Opera, 66
Phoebe Snow, 68
Soul Kiss, 82
Wedding Belle, 93
Weep No More, 93

Gin
Abbey Cocktail, 15
Alaska, 16
Allies, 16
Barbary Coast, 19
Barton Special, 20
Bloodhound, 22

Bronx Cocktail, 28
Bronx Silver, 28–29
Cabaret Cocktail, 29
Café de Paris, 30
Chocolate Soldier, 34
Claridge Cocktail, 34
Clover Club Cocktail, 35
Damn-the-Weather
  Cocktail, 36
Dempsey Cocktail, 36
Dixie Cocktail, 38
Dubonnet Cocktail, 38
Fino Martini, 40
Foghorn, 41
Frankenjack Cocktail, 42
Froth Blower Cocktail, 43
Gibson, 44
Gilroy, 44
Gimlet, 44
Gin and Tonic, 45
Gin Daisy, 45
Gin Fizz, 45
Gin Rickey, 45
Golden Dawn, 47
Grapefruit Cocktail, 47
Green Dragon, 48
Hasty Cocktail, 49
Hawaiian, 49
Hoffman House, 50
Imperial, 52
Jamaica Glow, 53
Jewel, 54
Jockey Club, 54
Judge, Jr., 54
Knockout, 54
Leapfrog, 56
Little Devil, 56
Long Island Iced Tea, 56
Maiden's Blush, 58
Martinez, 59
Martini, 59
Melon Cocktail, 60

113

Merry Widow, 60
Opera, 66
Orange Blossom, 66
Paisley Martini, 66
Paradise, 67
Parisian, 67
Park Avenue Cocktail, 67
Peach Blow Fizz, 68
Pink Gin, 69
Pink Lady, 69
Princeton, 71
Racquet Club, 72
Ramos Gin Fizz, 72
Red Cloud, 72–73
Rolls-Royce, 74
Royal Gin Fizz, 74
Royal Smile, 74
Russian Cocktail, 76
Singapore Sling, 81
Sloe Gin Fizz, 82
Snowball, 82
Star Daisy, 83
Stinger, 83
Straight Law Cocktail, 84
Tango, 85
Third Degree, 87
Tom Collins, 88
Tropical Cocktail, 89
Ulanda, 90
Victor Cocktail, 91
Wedding Belle, 93
White Lily, 94
White Rose, 95
Xanthia, 96

No-Alcohol Drinks
Angostura Cocktail, 101
Cajun Tomato, 101
Fizzy Lemonade, 102
Hot Tomato, 102
Lime and Coke, 102
No Rum Rickey, 102–103
Orange and Tonic, 103

Orange Cooler, 103
Piña Non Colada, 103
Shirley Temple, 104
Tomato Mexicano, 104
Tomato and Tonic, 104
Unfuzzy Navel, 104
Virgin Mary, 105

Pernod
Duchess, 39
Suissesse, 85
White Way, 95
Yellow Parrot, 96

Port
Betsy Ross, 20
Broken Spur, 28
Chicago Fizz, 34
Coffee Flip, 35
Elk's Own Cocktail, 39
Glogg, 46
Japanese Fizz, 53
Mulled Claret, 64
Tempter Cocktail, 86

Rum
Acapulco, 15
Apricot Lady, 18
Bacardi, 18
Baltimore Eggnog, 19
Banana Daiquiri, 19
Barbary Coast, 19
Beachcomber, 20
Between the Sheets, 21
Bolero, 23
Bull's Milk, 29
Cardinal Punch, 31
Casablanca, 31–32
Chicago Fizz, 34
Daiquiri, 35
Derby Daiquiri, 37
Devil's Tail, 37
El Presidente, 40

Eye-Opener, 40
Fish House Punch, 40–41
Frozen Daiquiri, 43
Grog, 48
Hop Toad, 50
Hot Buttered Rum, 51
Hurricane, 51
Irish Shillelagh, 52
Jamaica Glow, 53
Judge, Jr., 54
Liberty, 56
Little Devil, 56
Long Island Iced Tea,
    56–57
Mai Tai, 57
Mary Pickford, 59
Parisian Blonde, 67
Piña Colada, 68
Planter's Punch, 69
Planter's Punch No. 2, 69
Poker Cocktail, 70
Quarterdeck, 71
Rum and Coke, 75
Rum Martini, 75
Rum Screwdriver, 75
Rum Sour, 76
September Morn, 79
Sevilla, 79
Shanghai, 80
Sir Walter Raleigh, 81
Strawberry Daiquiri, 84
Tahiti Club, 85
Torridora Cocktail, 88–89
White Lily, 94
White Lion, 94–95
Zombie, 96–97

Rye
Cablegram, 30
Elk's Own Cocktail, 39
Fox River, 42
New York, 64
Rock and Rye Cooler, 73

Scotch
Barbary Coast, 19
Blood and Sand, 22
Bobby Burns, 23
Flying Scotchman, 41
Miami Beach Cocktail,
    60–61
Modern, 62
Morning Glory Fizz, 63
Remsen Cooler, 73
Rob Roy, 73
Rusty Nail, 76
Scotch Cooler, 78
Scotch Holiday Sour, 78
Scotch Mist, 78
Scotch Sour, 78–79

Sherry
Bombay Punch, 24
Polonaise, 70
Sherry Cobbler, 80
Sherry Twist, 80
Straight Law Cocktail, 84
Tuxedo, 89

Sloe Gin
Black Hawk, 21
Irish Shillelagh, 52
Love, 57
Modern, 62
Moulin Rouge, 63
Ruby Fizz, 74–75
San Francisco, 77
Sloe Gin Fizz, 82

Tequila
Chapala, 33
Long Island Iced Tea,
    56–57
Margarita, 58–59
Strawberry Margarita,
    84–85
Tequila Manhattan, 86

Tequila Old Fashioned, 86
Tequila Sour, 87
Tequila Sunrise, 87
Tequini, 87
Toreador, 88

Vermouth
Allies, 16
Americano, 17
Blood and Sand, 22
Bloodhound, 22
Bobby Burns, 23
Bombay, 24
Bronx Cocktail, 28
Bronx Silver, 28–29
Carrol, 31
Claridge Cocktail, 34
Duchess, 39
Froupe, 43
Imperial, 52
Jewel, 54
Knockout, 54–55
Manhasset, 58
Martinez, 59
Merry Widow, 60
Miami Beach Cocktail,
   60–61
Morning Cocktail, 62–63
Picon, 68
Rolls-Royce, 74
San Francisco, 77
Soul Kiss, 82
Tango, 85
Third Rail, 88
Vermouth Cassis, 90
Victor Cocktail, 91
Washington, 92

Vodka
Beer Buster, 20
Black Russian, 21
Bloody Mary, 23

Cape Codder, 30
Devil's Tail, 37
Flying Grasshopper, 41
Gypsy, 48
Harvey Wallbanger, 49
Long Island Iced Tea,
   56–57
Moscow Mule, 63
Russian Bear, 76
Russian Cocktail, 76
Salty Dog, 77
Screwdriver, 79
Soviet Cocktail, 82–83
Vodka and Tonic, 91
Vodka Gimlet, 91
Vodka Grasshopper, 91
Vodka Sling, 92
Vodka Stinger, 92
Warsaw, 92
White Russian, 95

Whiskey
Barton Special, 20
Black Hawk, 21
Boilermaker, 23
Derby Fizz, 37
Dinah Cocktail, 38
Frisco Sour, 42–43
Gloom Lifter, 46
Highball, 49
Horse's Neck, 50–51
Hot Brick Toddy, 51
Irish Coffee, 52
Irish Shillelagh, 52
Japanese Fizz, 53
Ladies' Cocktail, 55
Lawhill Cocktail, 55
Los Angeles Cocktail, 57
Manhasset, 58
Manhattan, 58
New York Sour, 65
Old Fashioned, 65

Paddy Cocktail, 66
Opening Cocktail, 65
Preakness, 71
Quebec Cocktail, 71
Rattlesnake, 72
Shamrock, 80
Seven and Seven, 79
Silver Bullet, 81
Temptation Cocktail, 86
Trois Rivières, 89

Whiskey Cobbler, 93
Whiskey Daisy, 94
Whiskey Sour, 94

Wine
General Harrison's
  Eggnog, 44
Mulled Claret, 64
Sangria, 77
Spritzer, 83

Topic Index

Alcohol, 98
  abstinence from, 98
  overindulgence, 98
Alcohol-free drinks, 101

Bar, stocking of, 4
Beer, 8, 9, 10, 109
  history, 9
  keg contents, 109
  serving, 8
  types of, 10
Bourbon, 9

Canadian Whisky, 9

Dips, 12
Drinking and driving, 99
Drinks, 4, 8, 101, 111
  indexed by key liquor,
    111
  most popular, 4
  neat, 8

  nonalcoholic, 101

Equipment, 2
  bar basics, 2
  blender, 2
  shaker, 2

Food with drinks, 12

Garnishes, 5
Glasses, 3
  beer, 3
  brandy, 3
  cleaning, 3
  cocktail, 3
  old fashioned, 3
  wine, 3
Guacamole, 14

Ice, 6
Intoxication levels, 99
Irish whiskey, 9

Liquor, 5
  estimating quantity
    needed, 5

Measurements, 109
Mixers, 5
Mixing drinks, 7

Nonalcoholic drinks, 101

Recipes, 12, 13, 15, 101
  alcohol-free drinks, 101
  drinks, 15

Easy Shrimp Treat, 13
Guacamole, 14
Hummus, 14
Three-Cheese Spread, 13
Rye, 9

Scotch, 9
Smoking, 99
Snacks, 12
Social responsibilities, 98

Whiskey, 9
Wine, 8, 9, 11